A ROOM WITH A DIFFERENT VIEW

First Through Third Graders
Build Community and
Create Curriculum

Jill Ostrow

Stenhouse Publishers, York, Maine

Stenhouse Publishers, 226 York Street, York, Maine 03909

Library of Congress Cataloging-in-Publication Data

Ostrow, Jill.
    A room with a different view : first through third graders build community and create curriculum / Jill Ostrow.
        p.   cm.
    Includes bibliographical references and index.
    ISBN 1-57110-009-1 (alk. paper)
    1. Education, Primary—United States—Case studies. 2. Nongraded schools—United States—Case studies. 3. Classroom environment—United States—Case Studies. 4. Ostrow, Jill.
    5. Primary school teachers—United States—Biography.   I. Title.
    LA219.078   1995
    372.24'1'0973—dc20   95-7913
                                                                                CIP

Published simultaneously in Canada by
Pembroke Publishers Limited
538 Hood Road
Markham, Ontario L3R 3K9
ISBN 1-55138-063-3

Cover and interior design by Ron Kosciak, *Dragonfly Design*
Typeset by Pre-Press Company, Inc.
Cover, interior, and insert photography by James Whitney.

Manufactured in the United States of America on acid-free paper
99 98 97 96 95 8 7 6 5 4 3 2 1

   Printed on recycled paper

Linda Zackowsky

A Room with a Different View

To the children I learn with

for imagining with me—way beyond the boundaries of what's possible

and to Grey

for teaching me the significance of that

Contents

Acknowledgments

The writing and research that went into this book are largely the result of the learning I have gained from my students over the years. In particular, I wish to thank the members of "Ostrow's Outrageous Island" for their opinions and ideas, their enthusiasm, their incredible imaginations, and their generosity with their work.

I have received a tremendous amount of support, directly and indirectly, from many others during the months I spent writing this book. I would like to thank:

The parents of all my kids for their constant and continual support.

Julia Peattie, Kirstin Tonningsen, Mary Dilles, Brenda Power, and Grey Wolfe for taking the time to read through drafts and offering advice and opinions.

Lynn White and Steve Eiseman for always believing, supporting, and understanding my philosophy of how children learn.

Michael Shay, Bob Carlson, Alice Cotton, Laura Merrill, Marilyn Seger, Judie Forsyth, and Kirstin Tonningsen, my support at work.

Jane Stickney and Susan Dunn for always being there for me.

Jim Whitney for his brilliance with a lens, his encouragement, and his perfection.

All my friends and family for understanding why I was a "hermit" for much of the year.

Philippa Stratton for her support, advice, humor, and vision.

Allyn Snider for understanding *everything*, for her intelligence, and for being on the same wave-length.

And finally, Ruth Hubbard. If it wasn't for Ruth, this book never would have made it out of my head onto paper! She was the first person who encouraged me, or should I say pushed me, to write. She was the first person who totally agreed with me about how children learn. She was the first person who made me realize that I wasn't really out in left field! She spent hours helping me change sentences and rephrase words, teaching me how to make my words sound the way I wanted them to. I am grateful for her professional wisdom and her beautiful writing, but mostly, for her friendship. (She just needs to work on her choice of cookies!)

1

Welcome!

"What's this going to be?" I asked Dave and Zack as they diligently tried to attach a narrow, four-foot box to the top of a table.

"It's the water purifier," Zack quickly answered. He was so excited, he could hardly contain himself. He continued to explain how the contraption worked, probably because he saw the stunned look on my face.

"Well, if we are on an island now, we'll need clean water, right?"

"Uh huh," I muttered.

"Well," Dave added, "this will take the salt out of the water and give us fresh drinking water." By now, a group of children was congregating around Zack and Dave's water purifier listening intently to their detailed explanation.

"And look here," continued Zack, "the top of it is a food dispenser. Hey, Josh, throw me over your coconut. I'll show you how it works." Josh handed Zack the coconut he was about to attach to his palm tree.

"If I put the coconut on the top like this, then it rolls down the food dispenser and lands in a bucket of fresh water. It cleans the food and also gives us clean water," Zack explained.

"Cool!" someone called from the crowd of children.

"We need fresh water and clean food if we are going to live here," Dave summed up. The children hung around Dave and Zack for a few more minutes and then dispersed.

When I had finished gazing at Dave and Zack's magnificent creation, I turned around and was struck by the chaos around me. The room was a disaster. Pieces of green and brown paper were flung over chairs, couches, and tables. Huge cardboard carpet tubes were being taped to the floor and rolls of duct tape were being passed about. I stood there staring at the mess—grinning from ear to ear.

We were creating an island community. The kids spent the first two weeks of school in September transforming the room into an island environment. Palm trees made out of tubes stood around the room, a meeting hut surrounded the two small couches and two soft chairs, and a flat paper ship was stapled out in the hall with an anchor connecting the ship to our room. Tropical birds hung from the lights, pineapple bushes sprang up from the floor, and monkeys swung from the branches of the palm trees.

As I stood there staring in awe at these six- through nine-year-old children, I wondered how I had come to the place in my career where I could look at this *apparent* chaos and see all the learning that was taking place. I realized, as I watched the children working their fingers to the bone to make palm leaves stand without flopping over, how much I valued the ideas of community, choice, challenge, independence, and respect. The children were working together to build a community. They made choices about the materials they used for their palm trees and about how they constructed them. They challenged themselves, as Zack and Dave had done with the water purifier. I saw how independent the children were as they worked—when they finished something, they went right on to make something else. And I saw how much children can respect each other, regardless of age or gender. Third graders and first graders, boys and girls, worked side by side. As I watched the children create our island community, I realized how much I had learned as an educator.

I am a teacher, but I am also a student and a teacher researcher. I am writing this book because I want to share with a larger audience all that my students have taught me over the last thirteen years I have been in the classroom. This book is *not* a "how-to" or "should-do" book. I am simply describing what works for me and my students. You may wonder whether or not the activities and projects in this book would work in your classroom. They probably wouldn't, but the *philosophy* underlying them would. This book is based on my beliefs about how children learn and the work that children do to support that philosophy. Many "how-to" books show teachers activities to use with all children in all classes. I want to demonstrate that the activities need to be different for individual children and for different classes. The philosophy is constant; only the ideas, activities, and projects change.

Even though the island community we were creating was make-believe, the community that was forming inside our classroom was very real.

"Why aren't you going out to recess, Zack?" I asked one afternoon just after the kids had gone outside.

"Oh, well, I broke the law. I was running in the lunchroom. Rachel gave me two minutes off my recess." Zack watched the clock, waiting for the two minutes to pass, and then ran outside to play. He had been given an "island consequence" set up by the Island Lawmakers, one of the six jobs the kids devised. The lawmakers came up with the laws for the island and brought them to the rest of us for approval. We voted on each law and were all responsible for following those laws throughout the year. If a law was broken and an island member saw it, the lawbreaker was given a "consequence." Why would one child accept a punishment from another? Because we were a community—created, built, and run by the children. Everyone respected the community as well as its laws. They knew what their choices were. Zack chose to run in the lunchroom. It was pretty hard for him to deny it in front of the twenty-four children who saw him, so he accepted Rachel's ruling to take time off his next recess. Three years ago, when he was a first grader in my class, if another child had told him to take time off his recess he would have laughed and run out to play. Although we focused on theme studies and integrated much of the curriculum then, our sense of community was not as strong as it is now.

Theme studies are great, but I have found that they need to be placed in a larger context. All the themes we followed up during the year of the island referred back to the idea of the island, and all related to our sense of community. Because Zack had been in my class for three years, he had been an active member in building our community, and accepting a consequence ruling from another child was not difficult for him.

Multi-aged classrooms are not just a progressive "fad" for the 1990s. When I started teaching at the Wilsonville Primary School three years earlier, I taught a straight first grade. The following year, I kept half that class and taught a first/second blend. The third year, the year of the island project, I was able to keep most of the kids going into the second and third grades (some of the remaining kids had moved). I just needed eight new first-grade children. I ended up with eight children at each of the three grade levels (although those numbers changed during the year because some kids moved away and others joined the class). The third graders were with me for their third year in a row. By now they knew the organization of the room so well, that September was the smoothest "back-to-school" transition I've ever experienced. The new first-grade children seemed a bit lost the first couple of weeks, but they soon fit in and began doing a level of work I had never seen from such young children.

Multi-aged classrooms, especially those like mine that span four years, demonstrate what children are able to do. They also break down barriers of age and gender. (First-grade girls actually invite third-grade boys to their birthday parties, not a usual occurrence in a straight grade.) The children learn to respect each other as individuals, *not* according to age or grade level. They learn to look at their classmates' progress almost as closely as I do. Grant, for example, often follows up on Anna: "Look Jill, I can read Anna's writing! I couldn't last year. Good job, Anna." Comments like these are heard constantly in this classroom. The children progress at their own rate so individual progress is easily seen. If I were to give my whole class the same worksheet, with the same answers, what would I—or the children—learn from each other? Yet, if I pose the same question to each child, and every answer is different, we all learn a tremendous amount. Multi-aged classrooms serve as one learning approach that encourages teachers to look at children as individuals—it's impossible to compare classmates who range in age from six to nine—and to compare children only to themselves. In terms of meeting individual needs, for me teaching a multi-aged class is no different than teaching a straight grade. The children in my straight first-grade class represented a huge range of abilities, so I adjusted my program to each child. The same holds true for a multi-aged class. Instead of reading "how-to" books, I look at children's learning process. If I understand that, teaching an age span of four years isn't any different from teaching a class of children who are all the same age.

Even so, I was a bit apprehensive that first September. I kept telling myself that I had always taught a class of children whose ability range was greater than four years, so why should this be different? Then I realized that I wasn't as concerned about academic differences as I was about social differences. At first, I was worried that the older children would resent having the younger children in the class. Looking back, that wasn't the case. Dave, a second-grade boy, was new to our class that year, but he was already good friends with some of the third graders. Everyone instantly adored Kyle, Josh's younger brother.

Josh was a third grader, and Kyle a first grader. That first week Kyle and Zack, a third grader, worked on a project together. They worked as equals, but if Zack needed to take over at a difficult point, he did so naturally and always made Kyle feel that he was an important member of their partnership.

The umbrella for everything we do in our class is the idea—and the feeling—of community. To have a class feel like a community goes beyond mere cooperative groupings. In a classroom community there is a feeling of respect all day long, every day of the school year. If the teacher always forms the children into groups, it will be difficult to create an environment of respectful learners. Children need to learn how to form their own groups. They need time to make choices about whom they work with and to form opinions about other children independently. This is true in a classroom community as well as in a school community.

Many elementary schools are working to bring together diverse philosophies, teaching styles, and personalities. These schools believe that one way to combat in-school tensions among staff is to come up with schoolwide themes. But in my experience, tensions won't magically subside just by choosing a schoolwide theme.

The key to building community is respect. Think about your own communities, both professional and personal. Whether they work—or don't work—depends on the mutual respect members have for one another. In the same way, children deserve respect as vital members of the school community. Yet this doesn't always happen. Instead, two separate communities develop within a school: the children in one, and the adults in the other. This troubles me.

I work hard to create an equal, respectful community within my classroom. My students know I respect them. They know I will listen to their ideas and opinions or to their side of an issue or argument. Yet they also realize how important a sense of community is to me. They know how strongly I feel about respecting others. As their teacher, I will make certain decisions that will affect them directly, but, because I also respect my children as tough, independent learners with strong opinions, they know they can question those decisions openly and be heard by someone with an open mind.

The children in my class also learn to be accountable for their behavior outside our classroom. If they are disrespectful to an adult or another child, they know they will have to answer to me as well as to their classmates. They know that their behavior directly affects the rest of the community. At the same time, they know they can discuss occasions when they feel they have been treated with disrespect outside the classroom.

Building community every year is essential. In the deepest sense, that is what this book is about. It shares with you how our community was developed, how it grew and changed over one school year and how the children became community builders and curriculum coordinators through the establishment of our island community.

When we decided as a class to build an island community, the first thing the kids wanted to do was to choose a name. We voted and "Ostrow's Outrageous Island" won. We had a name and an idea. Now what? I decided to ask the kids. I was committed to having us all build this community together. I didn't want to be responsible for making all of the decisions about curriculum; I wanted the children to be community builders and curriculum coordinators with me. Before we could begin talking about anything else, we needed to imagine what our community might look like. We needed a foundation. The kids came up with many good ideas. The first was to make the room look like an island, and we spent the better part of the first two weeks of school doing just that.

The kids worked in jobs that helped maintain the operation of the community. The jobs ranged from the garbage company to the bank. In Chapter 2 you will read about how we transformed our room and established jobs. The rest of the chapters show how everything we did that year revolved around our island community and how philosophy and teaching were woven together as we created our year-long curriculum. You will read about the physical aspect of our room in Chapter 3. The work the children participated in is outlined in Chapter 4. Chapter 6 talks about assessment. These things may look different from a conventional classroom, but the intent and outcomes are consistent with my philosophy of how children learn. I have spent years questioning why and what I've been doing, and I've tried to answer some commmonly asked questions by visitors and other educators in Chapter 7.

My classroom is not magically transformed into a perfect little community during the first or second month of the school year. It takes time to earn trust and respect. Children need to be able to make choices, become independent, and accept and create challenges for themselves. And they need to be able to make mistakes. The students in my classroom learn to disagree and support their disagreements with reasons. There needs to be room for disagreement among staff members, too. Unfortunately, many groups of teachers aren't comfortable disagreeing with one another. As adults, we should allow ourselves to make mistakes and have disagreements as we struggle to create a community of teachers. I find that talking about my concerns with the children helps me to evaluate my own perceptions. Often, I have judged an activity or a project as a failure, only to discover that the kids loved what they were doing. If I paid attention only to my perceptions, I wouldn't get the full picture. I also include the children in many curriculum decisions. That's not to say that I don't have an agenda. The island year described in this book was largely created by the children, but its *direction* and *intent* came from me.

Why are we doing this? It's a question I ask myself often. If I can't come up with a good answer about a particular activity, I give myself some options: I can talk to the kids to see if they understand why we are doing it; we can change it; or we can scrap it all together. Over my years of teaching, I have drastically changed many of the things I learned in my "teacher training" days. Just before I stopped giving spelling tests, for example, I asked myself, "Why do I do this? Are the children *really* learning how to spell better as they draft? Does giving children lists of words to memorize show them all the other spelling strategies that they could use? Aren't I only teaching to the middle?" When I sat down and answered those questions, I realized I was doing something I didn't believe in. I go through these questions for almost everything I do in my classroom and they have formed my philosophy of how children learn.

My questions have also been shaped by other educators. Ruth Hubbard, who appears throughout this book, has been a significant presence. The kids and I have been fortunate in having her in our classroom over the last three years as part of her own current research. Through our discussions I have been able to explore my philosophy of how children learn. We experiment together, formulating answers and then asking more questions. Ruth has shown me how to be a teacher researcher, how to learn from my observations of the children.

Another helpful person is Allyn Snider, who has been an important influence on my thinking about how children learn. Allyn and I are able to disagree, share our ideas, talk about the learning process, compare our work, and support each other's programs. Just as children gain information for their research projects by using more than just books, so do teacher researchers. I observe children and talk to and read books by other educators to help answer my questions. Through my observations and discussions, I have been able to create an environment in which I can put those beliefs into practice. This book is meant to serve as a window into a classroom with a *different* view.

"Okay, Jill. Dave and I have finished the water purifier. Now we can start drinking the water." And so began the year of the island.

2

The Island

TRANSFORMING THE CLASSROOM

How did we create our island community? In some ways we started from scratch. But the idea of changing the room wasn't new to the kids. Over the previous two years, for every topic we studied we transformed the classroom. The kids were eager to get going, so I went in to school over one weekend and put up blue and green butcher paper to signal to the kids when they came to school on Monday that we would begin. It was wonderful having so many of the same children for another year. They were able to jump right in and begin coming up with ideas. They knew immediately how to build the meeting hut, and the new children became their apprentices. The island hut played off the African huts we had made when we transformed the classroom into an African village. For these we had used carpet roll tubes, which are wonderful for building large structures. I bought about twenty twelve-foot carpet rolls at a carpet store. I took another teacher with me, and we spent about forty-five minutes sawing the rolls in half so they would fit into the car, but it was worth every minute. They are made of extremely strong cardboard and we use them constantly to staple into, tape to the floor, and stick wire through. These have already endured for two years (see insert page 1).

The kids were able to make a larger and stronger meeting hut because of their previous experience. This is one reason I like to keep children in my classroom for more than one year. The month of September is so much smoother when children are already familiar with each other, with me, and with the environment.

The children worked on making "things" for the island for the first two-and-a-half weeks of school. Alone and in small groups, they worked on the island project at the beginning and the end of the day, usually in twenty- to thirty-minute blocks. Because I wanted to encourage a community of respectful learners, I divided the kids into groups of three to begin working on the palm trees. This decision served two purposes: I wanted to observe the various multi-aged groups working together; and I wanted the kids to design their palm trees instead of just jumping in haphazardly. Together they were to come up with a plan and make a list of the materials they needed. The more experienced members of the group already knew about the carpet roll tubes, so everyone wanted a tube. The groups worked quite well together on that small project. Although the older children seemed to take over the bulk of the designs, some of the younger kids also chimed in with their ideas.

"Jill, look at Sharat's cool way to make a palm leaf!" Tessia, a second-grade girl, was excited about Sharat's leaf. A group of children ranging in ages from six to nine began to congregate around Sharat.

"Cool!"
"How'd you do that?"
"That's a neat way to make a palm leaf."
"That's good for a first grader."
"It's neat, but I still like my way. Come on, let's go."

These comments reassured me that the kids could look at new ideas with open, noncompetitive minds. I was a little taken aback by the comment "good for a first grader." "Of course he has good ideas," I thought to myself. "What does age have to do with that?" I would hear more comments like these throughout the first few months of school, but by November, age and grade level were rarely brought up. By then, the kids were looking at each other as individuals, not as kids in different grades.

All the palm trees looked different. Instead of spending an hour explaining to the kids how to make palm trees, I left the designs up to them. They had many problems to solve as they began following their plans for the trees.

"We're ready for our tube, Jill," shouted Joshua.

"Okay, but remember last year, how we drilled holes into the top of some of the tubes so we could put string through them and attach the string to the lights so they'd stand up? Well, I couldn't see very well in the dark basement, so the tubes I grabbed don't have holes in them. It's up to you and your group to figure out how to attach the leaves to the tube and make the tube stand up."

"Oh, brother!" Joshua sighed as he trotted off to solve this new problem.

I played soft island music throughout the time we worked on transforming our classroom into the island. But the kids did not sit quietly cutting out leaves. The room was a mess and it was noisy. (When is true learning *not* messy?) If the children hadn't felt free to move around the room, they would not have been able to share ideas. If I had explained how to make a palm tree, we wouldn't have ended up with such a variety. I encouraged the children to use their knowledge and their imagination. Sharat's palm tree looked quite different from the rest. The kids walked around observing how other groups had designed their leaves and either got ideas for their own or offered comments, as did I.

"Bekka, your leaves are so huge. How will they stay up?"

"I don't know."

"Well, they need to be able to stay up and not flop over. What could you use to help the leaves do that?"

"Um, how about cardboard?"

"Oh, that sounds good. It might work. I was thinking of using wire, but the cardboard might work. Try that first. Be sure to let me know what happens."

Eventually, Bekka and her group ended up using both cardboard and string to hold up the leaves.

While we prepared our island environment, we were also creating a story about how we came to be there. We took some time just to talk about the story, but we didn't write anything down at first. We were simply gathering ideas and playing with possibilities. We pretended that we had started out on a ship that ran into a terrible storm and was wrecked on a small island. We would later write down the final story explaining our arrival (see Figure 1).

As the class attended to their island projects during that first week of school, the idea of community hovered constantly in the back of my mind. I observed how the children worked together and tried to think of ways to support community growth. A parent of two of the children in my class suggested an interesting idea: the children were to think of a special quality about

We were sailing in the Pacific Ocean when a storm came. Some lightning hit our ship, and we crashed into an island! We took the anchor of the ship and put it on the shore of the island so the ship wouldn't float away.

It was a deserted island. We named it *Ostrow's Outrageous Island.* Then we built a meeting hut out of grass and palm leaves. There was a storm that knocked down a palm tree, and it came crashing into the hut! So we used the wood to make a table. We patched the roof up with palm leaves.

We also built a small hut to use as our Information Center.

We, the 28 people that sailed on that ship, are between 6 and 33 years old and 3 to 5 feet tall. We each brought with us a special gift. Here we left the boat with pictures of us. We now inhabit *Ostrow's Outrageous Island* and share with you the gift we brought with us.

We have been building and creating a livable community and invite you to visit our island.

We hope to return to Wilsonville sometime in the middle of June!

FIGURE 1   Here is the story of our arrival at "Ostrow's Outrageous Island."

themselves—a "gift"—that they brought with them to the island. Then they made half-size body pictures of themselves out of paper to illustrate their gift. A lot of different ideas grew out of this project.

JB, an older child, asked right away for a yardstick. "What are you going to use the yardstick for?" I asked him.

"I need to measure myself and divide that in half. What else?" I felt silly for asking! On the other side of the room, a group of kids were putting row after row of unifix cubes together.

"Hey, what are you guys doing?"

"We're going to see how many unifix cubes tall we are and then break the line in half." Others got string and measured themselves, folded the string, and then cut it in half. All of these ideas originated with the kids. I offered no suggestions about how to do the assignment. They were experimenting with measurement, and from those experiments came new ideas.

After they had colored in their body pictures and cut them out, I asked the children to tell me the gift they had thought of. Kyle's gift was his drawing, Anna's her kind heart. It was difficult for some of the kids to come up with a "gift."

"I can't think of anything," Chris told me.

"Oh, of course you can. Just think," was my very unhelpful-helpful answer.

"Um, I don't know," and off Chris walked looking quite bewildered. Later that day, he came running up to me and beamed, "I have a good gift now. Kyle told me my writing is good. He said I should use that as my gift." My point here is that the children helped each other. The "gifts" varied from academic to social: Laura's was her descriptive writing, JB's baseball, Josh's caring about people, and Chris's his writing. Mine was my wild imagination.

I had wanted to find a way for the younger children to feel part of this already close-knit class. This assignment allowed the new children to realize early on that each of them had a special gift to offer the rest of the group, if not drawing, then having a "kind heart" or being a "good friend." I wanted all the children in the class to feel that they were able to contribute something to the community. I wanted them to know that, in this world of constant labeling, they *all* were gifted and talented.

For days, while some of the kids were busy building the meeting hut and the palm trees, others were making a huge boat to hang in the hall outside our classroom. They were using brown butcher paper, some shaping sails, others helping to cut out the huge ship. The hall wall outside my classroom is divided by my door, about twelve feet of wall space to the left, and about a foot of wall, then a drinking fountain, then four or five more feet of wall to the right. The finished boat stretched along the entire space on either side of the door and stood about five-feet high in the center. We cut a hole for the water fountain and another one for our door. Then I stapled the kids' body pictures onto the boat so it looked as if we were standing on the deck, and we mounted the gift sentences next to or on the picture. Our story, typed and mounted, was put up at the far end of the boat so people walking by could read it (see Figure 2 and insert page 2).

Dave cut an anchor out of cardboard and threaded a piece of rope through a hole he made in the top. He attached the cardboard anchor from the boat out in the hall to the closet inside our room, explaining that if we didn't have an anchor we'd float away. He would "drop anchor" every morning.

Looking through the doorway into the classroom that first week, you would have seen kids busily making palm trees, birds, coconuts, and a hut. The kids continuing from the previous year, who remembered how to make huts because of our African village, were helping to make the "meeting hut" for our island community. We put one carpet roll tube on either side of the couches in the middle of the room. Jim Whitney, the incredible photographer who took the pictures for this book, had left a roll of gaffers tape behind the year before. (Little did he know that when something as useful as that tape is left in our room, you can pretty well kiss it good-bye.) Needless to say, we used this strong tape to attach the tubes to the floor. Someone had the idea of stringing wire across the fluorescent lights that hang down from the ceiling to form the roof of the

FIGURE 2 The boat in the hallway outside of our classroom.

hut and keep the tubes from falling over. (They stayed up all year, but I did rip six floor tiles up when we took them down in June. Maybe that tape was a bit *too* strong!) I was in charge of connecting the wire across the lights. Almost everyone else was busy making leaves to lay across the wire for the ceiling of the hut.

When it was time to mount the leaves on the wire, I stood on a table and the kids handed their leaves up to me. At one point, nine or ten kids came walking over with a huge green leaf over their heads. They had made it together. When the roof was completed, we all sat inside the hut looking at our work. I asked, "Why do we need this roof?"

Tessia said, "It's so hot, and we need shade."

Someone else said, "And it could rain. We need protection."

I asked, "Why not just make it out of wood?"

Joshua said, "This is a tropical island. There're palm leaves."

I asked, "Why not oak leaves?"

Joshua answered very matter-of-factly, "'Cause this is a tropical island! There're no oak trees here!"

Alan added, "Also, palm leaves are better because they're bigger than oak leaves." Joshua was so sure about the tropical environment, while Alan's comparison of the size of the leaves showed his interest in detail, accuracy, and authenticity.

The room looked just the way we wanted it to look—like an island. I have found that the physical environment in the classroom is very much a part of the curriculum. If we did not spend time transforming the classroom to look like an island, we wouldn't have felt as if we were on an island. It isn't enough to study a theme or a topic and put together books containing the kids' work. We need to feel as if we are actually experiencing what we are learning about. This goes way beyond "hands-on." Planning and building a physical environment allows children to gain experience and express their creativity and imagination. They created and lived on the island for nine months. It was theirs.

Zack wasn't making palm trees or helping with the hut or the boat. He was concerned about the salt from the ocean, so he was building a water purifier out of a five-foot-long rectangular box. At the base of the purifier was a "coconut" with holes in it. This is what caught the salt but let the fresh water flow through. The water purifier also had a food dispenser attached to it. Food could be placed on top of the box to be cleaned by the water flowing through it. On the food dispenser Zack had posted a sign.

> This is A Food Despesor.
> And This is How it works
> The Food roles Down the Tube
> and in to the Basket oF
> water and cleans it oFF.
> so wee have cLean FooD.

There was another sign next to this one that read:

> DO not toch
> and i mene
> DO not tach

I never told Zack to make either the water purifier/food dispenser or the signs. This is what happens when a child's imagination and creativity encounter the *experience* of an idea. Because of Zack's invention, we were all able to learn about salt water and why his water purifier was so vital to us on the island. Zack also reminded me of the importance of play. He was a third grader, but even third graders need time to play. Children stood around the food dispenser watching it work. Some of them laughed and giggled as they sent fruit down the food dispenser chute to see if it would fall into the basket. Kyle even pretended to eat his pineapple after he had sent it down the food dispenser. It was easy for us all to imagine water rushing through this invention and being trapped by a make-shift coconut at the bottom.

The children's imaginations played a vital role in their creation of the island. JB insisted that there wouldn't be chairs and that we should cover them all with paper and turn them into rocks. I asked if we could just *imagine* that instead of actually doing it! But the fact that he could think of it made me realize again how important imaginative play is. There is a blue rug under the L-shaped, two-step platform we built last year for the room, and the kids would often pretend it was a lagoon.

From Zack's idea came others. Rachel and Laura made kayaks. They also pushed two desks up against the wall, covered them with paper and created a small hut called the "Info Center." This was meant to be a central place where people could go for information. Dave and Joshua made a rescue helicopter and put it up on the wall, and Alan made a pineapple bush. Grant and JB made a waterfall out of blue crepe paper. It started on the wall and cascaded down over the top of the cabinet where the kids' work boxes sat. Carly and Morgan made a flamingo. Larry, Alan, and Torin were making something out of a plastic lid, rope, and tape. When Larry was asked what it was, he said, "It's a trap to catch small animals." Alan added, "It couldn't catch Morgan's flamingo, but it could catch small animals." The kids made things by drawing on what they already knew about tropical islands. We had not done any further research on tropical islands at that point, yet their questions often sparked good research questions. One day, Mariah asked Ruth, "Are there frogs on tropical islands?"

Ruth replied, "I don't know. How could you find out?"

Anna, who was listening, answered, "You could get a book at the library. Like one that's all about tropical islands. I'll go with you."

And the two girls headed to the library to answer their question. Zack asked if moss grew on palm trees. He also went to the library to find the answer. I let the children play with their knowledge and their questions.

The children's sharing of their ideas for making things for the island was phenomenal. I never heard children complaining that someone was copying an idea. I never saw children sitting around not helping, although I did see children taking breaks from working and taking time off to think up new ideas. Megan whined about not wanting to make a leaf. I simply said, "Okay, but you'll be awfully bored." A few minutes later, off she went to make a leaf. I saw younger children helping older children and older helping younger. Working together like this was a first step in creating a community of respectful learners.

It may seem that all this movement and noise in the classroom produced a chaotic mess, but it was very important to allow the children this less structured time to create independently and walk around the room freely discussing their ideas and expressing their opinions. At the same time, the room was very structured in that the kids knew exactly what was expected of them.

I began to feel a bit anxious about spending so much time on making things for the island, so I decided to try to steer our focus a little bit. I had reminded the children before they began their island work what their responsibilities would be. One morning before we began discussing the community, I opened by saying, "You may continue working on what you need to do for the island. This is the last day to make 'things': boats, birds, waterfalls. This afternoon, we'll be working on our community. Nobody, nobody, nobody should be sitting here not working. What can you do if you've finished one project?"

Someone answered, "Do another bird."

Someone else said, "Make something else."

This was when Dave had the idea for the helicopter. "Maybe an airplane with a rescue sign overhead."

I said, "Great! I love it. Go to it."

The kids' ideas were their way of forming a community on their own. Rachel and Laura's Info Center was an important aspect of the island community; they realized that a community needed a central place for visitors to come with questions or concerns. Dave and Grant were looking out for the interests of the entire community by making the rescue helicopter. Zack was concerned about having fresh water for all of us. Our community was forming before I even realized it was happening.

In addition to the physical environment, we needed to create a livable, workable community *together*. I wasn't totally sure how to go about this, so I decided to ask the kids.

CREATING THE ISLAND COMMUNITY

The Job Groups

One afternoon we met and talked about what makes a community run smoothly. I asked the children to think about what types of things their town of Wilsonville, Oregon, had that enabled it to function as a community. They came up with the following list:

garbage	government	roads
housing	newspapers and telephones	banks
stores	schools	Burger King
Taco Bell	post office	grocery store

From this list, which I recorded on our white board, we chose those we thought were the most important for our island community. Then I had the kids sign up for a group they were interested in. I asked the oldest to choose first and to spread themselves out among the various groups. That seemed to work well, and I have used this method in other situations when I want to be sure to get a good mixture of students. The way the kids choose partners or groups varies with the project or problem and with my expectations or intentions for the activity. Sometimes I'll simply say, "Find someone who is different in either age or gender from yourself." At other times I may ask them to choose someone they have never worked with before. When they met in their groups that day, I asked them to come up with a name and then to decide how their job would help our island community.

The final job committees and their chosen names were

Ostrow's Outrageous Garbage Company
Island Lawmakers
Ostrow's Outrageous Planning Commission
Island Department of Housing
First Island Bank
The Island Times

The children shared the names easily when we met back on the platform (where we gathered for group meetings), but when it came time to share how their jobs would help the community, their faces were blank. I knew we needed to have some discussions. For the next few days we talked about why each job was important in running a community and how that job could help the community. I decided to also give each job group a goal before they met together a second time. Every morning, for thirty to forty-five minutes, we met in job groups. Each group had a "job folder" in which they kept all their notes and jotted down ideas. I roved the room listening in on the conversations. Every time we did "Island Work," we wore our "job" shirts, bright T-shirts a parent and I had made that said "Ostrow's Outrageous Island" across the front and had space for us to write our names on the back. They added to our sense of community as we worked together, each job group on its specific goal.

Ostrow's Outrageous Garbage Company

"Why don't we take the garbage out in the afternoons?" asked Chris.

"Well, where should we take it?" responded Kiersten.

"The dump!" shouted Chris.

"We can't go to the dump. We don't have a car." Anna replied.

"Well, I know, why don't we just find out where the garbage gets tooken out?" said Kiersten.

"Yeah, let's do that. And we need to make a clean-up day too. How about Wednesday?" Anna added.

I asked the garbage company to think about the following questions:

1. Where does the garbage get taken?
2. What time of day will you need to take the garbage out?
3. Who will take it out?
4. How will Craig, our custodian, know we took the garbage out?
5. What else in the room needs cleaning?
6. How much of Craig's time will be saved by our cleaning?

The garbage company came up with a system for cleaning the room and taking out the trash. They decided that Wednesday would be clean-up day, the one day they actually took our cans out to the bins at the side of the school.

Unfortunately, this caused a problem with the custodian, who didn't want the kids doing his job. He had caught them on their first Wednesday and was angry that they were throwing trash away out by the dumpsters. I was a bit puzzled by his reaction. I had just assumed that he would like a little help, but later I realized the foolishness of my decision. I certainly should have talked to him first and explained why and how the kids would be doing this little job (a lesson I have learned for future projects!). Needless to say, we modified that responsibility so that the kids gathered up the two classroom trash cans and set them close to the room door at the end of the day.

The garbage company was also considering cleaning up parts of the playground. They spent part of their job group meeting trying to come up with a reasonable and appropriate plan.

Island Lawmakers

"If someone breaks one of the laws, they'll have to write fifty sentences," said Grant.

"That doesn't make any sense, Grant," argued Dave.

"Yeah, why should a first grader have to write the same amount as a third grader?" added JB.

"No, I mean it doesn't make sense to have to write sentences. We shouldn't make anyone work like that for breaking a law," Dave explained.

"I think a better consequence should be having to miss time off of a recess. Let's take away something everyone likes," Tessia suggested.

"Yeah, like five minutes off recess for the first time, and then all recess and then you have to miss mini-classes. Everyone likes recess and mini-classes, so who would break a law?" Dave concluded.

The questions I asked the lawmakers to consider were the following:

1. What types of laws will you make?
2. What will the consequences be?
3. How will we vote on the laws?
4. What happens if the laws you made are voted down?
5. Who will enforce the laws?
6. Do the laws apply only to this classroom?
7. What about outside the classroom?

The lawmakers worked at coming up with laws—and appropriate consequences for breaking them—for the class to vote on. They thought of some good ones as well as some pretty silly ones. (My favorite was one Dave suggested: go with the flow. It was interesting to watch that law being enforced!) The kids were also playing around with the idea of consequences, and their discussions were extremely interesting to observe. They decided to take time off the recess break of kids who had broken an island law. The class responded well to these penalties and rarely had disagreements.

Toward the middle of the year, the lawmakers began holding mock trials. It was fascinating to watch them. I couldn't figure out how they knew the terms *plaintiff* and *defendant,* but several of them told me about a courtroom television show they had seen. The kids made up situations. There were two lawyers and each lawyer would take his or her client off to discuss trial strategy. When they returned, about two minutes later, the trial began. The judge sat in front and the lawyers presented their cases, questioning the defendant and plaintiff.

LAWYER: Well, why did you take the ball away from her?
DEFENDANT: I didn't. It was my ball and I wanted it back.
LAWYER: Well, why didn't you just ask her for it instead of grabbing it from her?

When they were finished, the judge would go off and come back with a decision, again, about two minutes. The children never did experiment with a jury; the judge was the sole decisionmaker in these mock trials.

The lawmakers decided that if someone broke the law three times, they would need to go to court. No one ever did.

Ostrow's Outrageous Planning Commission

Rachel explained her phone conversation with the manager of the river boat company:

"She said that it would cost $5 a kid, but when I told her who I was she said, 'Hang on a minute,' and came back to tell me she could give it to us for $3 a kid! I think she thought it was cool that I was making the call. Anyway, we have to be at the boat by 8:30. Should the planning commission write a letter to the parents telling them that we need to be at school early that morning? Also, it will be a two-hour boat trip, she said, 9 to 11. We thought we could all bring a lunch and eat downtown after the trip. Can we? We'll write the letter after we talk to Larry about the money and vote on it. I know everyone will vote to go!

The questions I wanted the planning commission to think about were:

1. How can this room be better planned?
2. How can the shelves be more organized?
3. Where can supplies be kept?
4. How can we avoid losing so many pencils?
5. Where can the art and blocks go to give us more space?
6. What can be done about the back room (the coat room) to give us more space?

The planning commission looked at the layout of our classroom in order to come up with a system of organization that would make it run more smoothly. They also planned where the "roads" should go on our island and made a map to help them decide where to put the roads without taking out too many trees.

The planning commission was also in charge of organizing our river boat field trip down the Willamette River. They made the phone calls, reported back to us, and even wrote notes home to parents.

Island Department of Housing

Here are some questions Jacob prepared for his interview with the principal:

How much does it cost to have the pink walls?
Can it fit through the door?
Can staples go through it?
How can we get it on the wall?
Where can we get it?

Among the ideas the housing group was thinking about were:

1. How can we make the classroom walls better so we can put things up more easily?
2. How much will it cost?
3. How can we make the room cooler?

The housing committee was responsible for figuring out how to make the classroom walls more able to accept staples. When panels of heavy-duty bulletin board material were being put up in one of the hallways, I asked for the scrap pieces, each about 2 feet by 4 feet. The committee measured the classroom walls and also figured out how many nails we would need in order to put up the panels.

First Island Bank

"We already took a big field trip. We need pencils!" Larry wanted to find out what supplies were needed for the room, so he went around asking every member of the class. He then put the items in order according to the number of requests each item received, wrote up a final list, and reported back to the class. We talked about these items and Larry decided that we should use up the entire budget on the supplies.

I asked the bank to consider the following questions:

1. Our room has $200 left to spend on books or supplies; how will you keep track of this money?
2. How will you give out the money?
3. How will you make your decision about what to buy or not to buy?

The bank was in charge of our $200 classroom budget. Larry, the sole member of the bank job group, was an important member of the community, and he knew it. He created a budget sheet and kept a running account of the money we spent.

Because we didn't need to plan much for the bank, Larry often helped out in other job groups. When someone had a question about money, they went to him, but he discovered early on that he didn't need to do much work in this job.

The Island Times

"I'll go and interview the garbage company," Carly said to Laura.

"Okay, and I'll interview the planning commission to see what they are doing. Joshua, who will you interview?"

"I don't know, maybe the lawmakers. Yeah, I'll interview them."

"Okay," said Laura, "And Kyle, you and Caitlin work on the cartoons."

The newspaper group was considering the following questions:

1. How will you organize the newspaper?
2. What sections will you have in the paper?
3. How often will the paper be published?
4. How will you write it?
5. Who will put it together?
6. How will you distribute it to everyone?

The Island Times group was focusing on putting together a newspaper. They would act as reporters and go around interviewing the members of other groups to find out what was going on in their jobs. Laura and Joshua asked our assistant principal to help them figure out what computer program would look like a newspaper (see Figure 3).

Job Work

Each morning before the kids went off to work in their job groups, we all met so that I could ask each group exactly what they were going to do that day. When I gather students together in this way, it is more than just a quick check on what is happening; it is also a useful way for the rest of us to know what each group is working on. We are constantly sharing our ideas and opinions, but these sharing times occur not just for group work. They are also important for writing workshop, reading workshop, math, project work—everything. It is

---

ISLAND TIMES

First Edition

Ostrow's Outrageous Garbage Company

the garbage take-out day is Wednesday in
the afternoon.

LAWS:
Island Lawmakers

The laws are: Tell the truth, walk in halls, be quiet in the halls & go with the flow which means cooperating.

Grant likes working for the laws because it's fun and you get to be like a police man and stop people.

Dave likes working for the laws because it's cool and there's lots of laws.
Dave also thinks its fun also because you get to take time out of peoples recess.

They voted on these laws: Be respectful when it's not your turn to talk, please don't chew gum out side the class room & at lunch don't get up just to run around and to do nothing.

CONSEQUENCES

take time of of recess & no clubs for a week.

FIGURE 3 Work-in-progress on *The Island Times.*

a basic part of my philosophy that children not only need to learn about independence, interdependence, and respect, they also need genuine situations in which to practice working as a community.

Alan and Jacob wanted to ask Ms. Seger, our principal, about getting the bulletin board material for the walls. Jacob said, "Me and Alan are gonna go to the office with questions I'm writing down."

"What is that called?" I asked him.

"An interview."

"Right. Jacob is interviewing Ms. Seger about the walls. Remember that you'll also need to set up a time for the interview."

When the children were involved in their job groups, they worked seriously and thoughtfully. The work was meaningful to them, and it was genuine: jobs relating to the island were important to all of us as a community. The children knew that if they didn't "pull their own weight," they would be letting everyone down. They also knew that they would be accountable to the other members of their group. As they learned about being accountable, they also learned what it means to be a part of a whole community, not just an individual student in a class.

That's not to say that there weren't problems. Once, during a morning meeting, I told the planning commission, "Okay, you had trouble cooperating yesterday. Maybe we need to define 'cooperation.'"

Dave, from the lawmakers group, heard this and said, "It's like going with the flow." Dave was echoing a newly voted in law the kids could understand. Because they had voted their approval of that law, they felt strongly connected to its validity. "Cooperation" seemed to be a loaded word when I first said it, but when Dave added, "Go with the flow," eyes lit up. The children seemed to be saying, "Oh yeah, I get it now."

Within the job groups, the kids were learning how to organize themselves on their own. They were figuring out how to split up the work, conscious of each member's different strengths and abilities. The newspaper group assigned Caitlin and Kyle, two younger children, to work on the comics while the rest of the members did the interviews. In the planning commission, Rachel and Josh directed Megan and Torin to draw rather than write. The lawmakers acted like real lawyers when they were dividing up the work load:

Tessia said, "I'm working on making our logo."

JB reported, "I'm sort of thinking about how to vote on the laws."

Dave suggested, "We should split up the group. You two figure out the votes and me and him will find the laws. Okay? And Tessia, you just do the logos."

The children were learning that each job helped another. They were learning that they *couldn't* work without one another. The planning commission had to go to the bank to find out if we could afford the river boat trip. The bank then had to go to the lawmakers to find out about the voting laws. The bank wanted the community to vote on the trip and needed to know the process. What struck me so quickly is their discovery that it wasn't enough to just *be* in a job group, they needed cooperation from other job groups as well.

These job groups met every morning from September through the middle of November. I can't remember the exact date they stopped meeting. It just seemed natural not to meet so often. We continued to meet sporadically or when we had an issue to address to a specific group. The curriculum developed naturally through the jobs. During the middle of the year, as our supplies were slowly disappearing, I gave some of the kids Larry's supplies list and asked them to try to get prices for the listed items from more than one store if possible. Using that list, I then devised a homework problem: the kids were to come as close to $200 as they could. We chose the plan with the best prices that best fit our needs, and I went to the store and spent the money. This was relevant curriculum that served a purpose. The children helped in the decision making process for this assignment by working on a homework problem. The outcome—much-needed supplies. The kids all felt that they were involved in the running of our community.

Visitors to my classroom often ask me about behavior problems or "resource kids." "You don't seem to have any problem kids," they say. I get a kick out of that comment, which I have heard many times. I try to explain that I don't see children as "problems." If a child is not doing what he or she is supposed to be doing at a particular moment, I ask that child, "What are you doing?" The usual response is "Nothing." "You're right. What are you *supposed* to be doing?" And that is usually all I need to say. Because what we do is meaningful and purposeful, and the children feel invested in what they are working on, visitors see them actively engaged. I have noticed through my years of teaching and observing children that behavior problems usually occur when children are not invested in what they are working on—when it is not meaningful to them.

Another common comment from visitors is, "Everyone seems so busy working. How do you do that?" I'm sure if the desks were in neat rows and I insisted on silence, the students would not all be busy at their work. Yet I don't have a classroom of twenty-five "perfect" children. What I do have is a classroom of twenty-five children whom I respect. I understand "down time," or bad days. I understand that they need to move freely around the room to talk to their friends socially or to get or share ideas. Because I give children this respect, when I ask them for some quiet work time, they cooperate.

At times, I felt that things weren't going exactly the way I wanted them to. I wasn't sure if I really had a definite direction. When we got together to share our job work, however, everyone seemed to know what they were doing. This reaffirmed my notion that I don't always *need* a specific direction. I like to give children the minimum of direction and instruction and then sit back and watch them take off. If they find it hard to "take-off," I listen to their questions. The more questions they have, the more ideas they come up with. Giving them minimal direction also helped me to learn that it was okay to have groups that were not working well all the time. They needed to solve their own problems within their groups.

People often ask me what happens when someone just won't work in a group or an idea just doesn't pan out the way I want it to. These things do happen, but I don't look at them as failures. I see them as another opportunity to observe what is going on. I intervene very seldom. When Caitlin or Megan would not work in their groups, instead of having a long talk with them I would tell them they'd be bored if they didn't help. Their groups were angrier with them than I could have been. They learned firsthand what it means when not everyone contributes to a community. I remember one conversation during a morning meeting about the planning commission.

JILL: Remember how we talked about how everything works together? So, if you don't listen to the planning commission and you don't put your pencils away, where are we going to have to go to get more pencils?
KIDS: The bank.
JILL: What if the bank doesn't approve it?
KIDS: No pencils.
JILL: That's why it's really important that you listen and pay attention to this.
DAVE: What happens if the lawmakers don't pay attention?
JILL: Well, that's a bad thing. What happens when the president isn't doing what he's supposed to do?
RACHEL: Sent to jail.

That exchange sparked a long discussion about communities working together and listening to each other.

Our island community was meaningful because all the children played a part in developing and creating it. We would talk openly in the group sharing about the internal problems of certain groups. These "problems" inspired new laws and new discussion. The children were learning about community by *living* as a community. It was real, so it worked.

We didn't spend the entire day creating our island during those first weeks of school. We didn't work in the job groups the entire year. But we did weave our island theme into many other projects throughout the year. The curriculum developed from the idea of the island. I did not make it the main focus for everything we did—the kids still had writing, reading, and math workshop times—but, because of the island environment we had all helped to create, it was easy to remember that we were members of a community.

3

Transformations:
The Physical Environment

"What are we going to change the room into this year, Jill?" Joshua asked the very first day of school. The students who had been with me for a few years took it for granted that we would transform the room into what we were going to study. From an African village to a planetarium to an ocean to an island: if we can imagine it, we can do it! Transforming the room is important, but the physical environment goes beyond making palm leaves and huts.

MOVEMENT AND CHOICE

During 1990–1991 I taught in the British Infant School System. I was overjoyed to walk into my classroom and find tables rather than desks. I hate teaching in rooms with desks. Desks make *true* cooperative learning almost impossible. Cooperative learning isn't just working in groups; it is learning with others. Talking with others about what you are learning, asking questions, giving advice to others, and making choices about whom to work with are all essential to cooperative learning. The only effective way to accomplish this kind of learning is to support *movement* and *choice*. When children can choose where they work and whom they work with, asking them to work quietly or divide into groups becomes easier. They respect my requests because of the respect I show them when they make choices.

My colleagues are often surprised by the fact that I don't assign seats to the children in my class. "Oh, that would never work in my room," they say. "My students would only choose to sit with their friends and talk." I have found that by taking away the seating chart children learn about making appropriate choices. Sure, I have children who begin the year wanting to work near a friend. Don't we as adults go into new situations wanting to sit near someone we know? Children learn how to balance those times they need to work in a social environment and those times they need to work independently. Independence isn't just knowing how to choose a book or put a pencil away. Independence is knowing how and where to learn best. Children need to discover their own learning patterns. (Yes, even first graders can do it!)

"Jill, can I go to the library? I need to work on this story and it's on the computer and there aren't any left in here," Kiersten asked during Writing Workshop. She was writing a story using the computer and her story was on her disk. She knew her choices were to start a new piece or to find a computer to work on. She was beginning to assert her independence in order to help her learning.

Children who socialize often during workshop-type activities learn to balance their socializing. They learn what is and is not appropriate in these learning situations.

"Jill, Joshua won't stop talking and I can't do this."

"So, what do you need to do?"

"If I move, he'll follow me."

"Well, you need to think of your choices and decide which one will let you get your work done."

Dave had been having difficulty with Taylor for some time. Taylor really liked and admired Dave, but he didn't know how to show his admiration without irritating Dave. Over time Dave learned to discuss his concerns with Taylor, but he also learned where he could go to sit so that Taylor wouldn't follow him. I also intervened at times and asked Taylor to move to another work spot.

"Okay, I'll stop talking to Dave and work."

"Taylor," I said firmly, "When you can get something done sitting away from Dave, you can sit by him again. But right now, you're not making the right choice."

When children are allowed to choose where they sit, natural groups begin to form. Throughout the year, during Writing Workshop, partnerships and groups formed that I would never have imagined could work. Kathleen, Zack, and Kyle were working on a piece together in late May. Kathleen was a new second-grade girl in our class, Zack was a third grader, and Kyle a first grader. Josh, Carly, Torin, and Morgan, whose ages ranged from six to nine, were working together on a poem book for about three weeks. The age barrier was gone in my room and the gender barrier was fading, and it happened naturally because of the children's mutual respect for each other. Had I forced this through seating charts or always grouping the children myself, I doubt that some of these groupings would have been possible.

Real learning requires movement. How, for example, could anyone learn to garden without movement? I have recently been learning to garden. I can't imagine having someone lecture to me about it without getting my hands dirty. Or a staff development session—wouldn't it be better to be involved in some way instead of just sitting and listening? For someone like me, who depends on movement for sanity reasons, I know how important this is!

When I showed slides of the classroom to the parents of my children last year, I explained why the kids don't have assigned seats. Kids were sitting all over the room, standing over desks, and even sprawling out on the floor. Some parents commented, "Oh, yeah! Now I see why!" The more comfortable we are, the more open we are to learning. Kids can't sit all day long—kids *shouldn't* have to sit all day long—and certainly not in the same uncomfortable seat.

FURNITURE AND FLOOR PLAN

I am beginning to collect round wooden tables to replace the Formica school tables. Besides the tables, over the years I have accumulated couches and chairs. In the summer of the year of the island I bought two small couches at a thrift store for $15. I had also bought a small square wooden coffee table. (The kids would sometimes sit on the floor and use a chair for a table, so I thought they'd like it.) A friend gave me another couch and two big chairs. I bought large throws that I could bring home to wash every now and then to cover the couches and the chairs. I was concerned about head lice, but the covers offered convenient protection.

I also have an L-shaped platform in my room. A friend of mine had visited schools in Italy and had noticed wooden platforms in many of the rooms. She explained to me over the phone from Chicago how she and her class had made one, and I decided I had to have one too.

I posed the following question to the children to go home and think about: "What size does our step need to be?" The next day, everyone had different answers depending on their experiences with measurement.

"I think it should be as big as an oatmeal box," said someone.

"I measured our stairs. They were each about a foot."

"And how big is a foot? What does a foot look like?" I asked. The next day, the child who wanted the step to be the size of the oatmeal box brought in an actual box. When he measured it, it came out to be a foot. So the step of our platform is indeed "the size of an oatmeal box." The kids measured and made plans and ended up actually building a mock platform out of poster board. It was huge: 6 by 2 feet for the top step and 6 by 4 feet for the bottom step. They even made blueprints for the actual platform.

A parent took the wood—donated by the principal's husband—and the blueprints to his home and began building the platform in four sections. (The sections make moving it easier.) When the sections were completed and set where we wanted them, I thought of carpeting, but I knew the cost was over our budget. The kids decided to write letters to the local carpet store asking them to donate the carpet. We talked about why we needed carpeting.

"Our butts get sore," offered Rachel. It was true! Without carpeting, the surface was quite hard.

"We want it to look nicer and we worked hard," another student commented. So, I took their letters explaining how hard the platform surface was and that "we don't even care what color carpet you give us, but we'd really like blue," to the local carpet store. How could the owner resist? He couldn't. The carpet he gave us wasn't blue, but it was free. He even came and installed the carpet on the platform during the day, so we could watch.

The platform serves a number of purposes: it is a great meeting place, a presentation stage, and a quiet working area. This year, I put one of the donated couches on the far side of the platform to make an even more enclosed area. I put the two small couches in an L-shape in the middle of the room with the coffee table in front of them. I also put two of the soft chairs in that area. I wanted the kids to walk in and see comfort, not desks. "This room looks like my living room!" one parent commented to me at the start of the year, and that's just what I want to hear. The furniture in the classroom is there as an extension of the curriculum. It is comfortable and invites learning and choice.

The way the furniture is arranged in my room not only encourages choice, it also allows easy access to supplies. The children know where the supplies are, how to get to them, and what is available to them. They can get their own paint, find the other materials they want to work with, and file away much of their own work. This is possible because of the way the room is set up and because I encourage them to be independent learners.

I have accumulated a huge library of over five hundred books during the past twelve years. They are stored in plastic tubs, sorted alphabetically by the author's last name, one tub for every letter of the alphabet. The children's published books are also kept in these tubs, arranged alphabetically by last name. I do not separate the children's published pieces from the other books. They are *all* authors. The kids can choose to read these books as well as books from the library. One reason I keep the books in tubs is for flexibility. When we transform or rearrange the room, shelves and supplies need to be easy to move.

The room also has several free-standing shelves that can be moved around easily. At the back of the room, an old coat room area we call the back room takes up valuable space. At the other end, on a back counter that stretches the length of the room, is a sink. An open shelf built into the wall in the back corner has become the art shelf. We keep paper in open tubs on the back counter as well as regular pencils, colored pencils, large and small markers, scissors, and glue. I do not let the kids keep cubbies anymore. The cubbies, which are located in that small back room, tend to become personal garbage cans, so we decided to use them for storing supplies.

When I took the cubbies away, I needed to get something for the kids to keep their work in, so I bought a storage box for each child—the cardboard magazine storage boxes that come in packages of three. The kids keep their writing folders, books they are reading, a clipboard, and any other work they are doing in their storage box. These, too, are flexible for easy movement. Flexibility is really the key to making the classroom function as I want. When we transformed the room into an African village, the kids needed to figure out where to put the supplies. One solution was inside one of the baobab trees we had made by tipping one of the shelves on its side and covering the whole thing with brown paper. The limbs of the tree, which stretched out from the trunk, were butcher paper that was rolled into tight branches.

"Hey, look here!" yelled Zack, "We can just cut a hole in the paper and make a door and put the pencils inside the trunk!" When someone has the idea of tipping over a shelf to use for a tree, they also know that the supplies in that shelf will need an alternative spot easily accessible to all of us. If the furniture were not flexible and movable, projects such as the African village or the island would not be possible.

BUILDING WITH—AND FROM—THE CURRICULUM

Hills and Mountains

During our study of the island's natural environment, some of the children were doing research on hills, mountains, and plateaus. We decided to make a hill and mountain for our island. Another class in my district had made a 3-D type structure like the one I wanted to make for our project. They used chicken wire to form the shell of the structure and then put papier-mâché over it.

I went in with a parent on a Saturday to put the chicken wire up. I didn't want the kids handling it and that turned out to be a wise decision; I had small cuts from the wire on my hands and arms by the time we had finished (a helpful hint: use gloves!). I wanted the entire structure to span the length of the wall. The height of the hill section extended to three feet below the ceiling and the adjoining cone-shaped mountain almost touched the ceiling. To create the shape, we stretched the wire over shelves and desks piled on top of one another. I had to nail part of the chicken wire to the wall to make sure it would stay up. I took the set of shelves that has a top and a bottom but no back or front, turned it on its side and used it as the "trapdoor" into the hills. Many supplies and materials were going to be stored inside, so we needed to figure out a way for the kids to have easy access to them. We put chicken wire over this shelf, and I used wire cutters to cut away the part that would be the door.

At its other end, the mountain reached just below the ceiling. Its end rested on top of a file cabinet that was to become the second opening into the structure (see insert page 3).

On Monday, the kids and I began putting papier-mâché onto the chicken wire. We used wallpaper paste and the newspapers we had been collecting for a week. I had never done this kind of project before and was a bit discouraged when the paper kept slipping off the oily wire. We finally figured out that if we could get a few pieces to stay, the rest would stick to it. When we finished, the room was a mess, but even though it took an hour to scrub the glue off the floor, it was worth every scrub.

The mountain was huge, six feet high and about twelve feet across, and protruding about four feet into the room. We let the structure dry overnight and would begin painting it on Tuesday. (I had thought it would take a good three days to papier-mâché this huge structure, but it only took a few hours. Three kids worked at a time using whole sheets of newspaper.)

On Tuesday, we talked about colors. The kids mixed various shades of green and brown. Before they began painting, I told them to be sure to mix their paint with that of the person next to them to blend the colors in. At one point that morning, twenty-five children were painting at once.

"How are we going to get the top, Jill?" someone asked. Good question. I couldn't even reach it with a ladder because it came out so far from the wall. Then I thought of some long, six-foot dowels left over from a former project. We taped paint brushes to the dowels and that seemed to have worked fairly well. We couldn't get to the very top with paint, so I tossed some green crepe paper up to hide the chicken wire.

On Wednesday, after the whole structure had dried, the kids began making things to go on top of the hills. Megan made a cardboard deer, a group of kids made a rabbit family, others made flowers, and Anna and I painted a river on the side where the mountain was. I took their work boxes out from inside the structure and placed them outside the mountain opening (see insert page 3).

Planetarium

The hills and mountain and the African village were huge, demanding projects to undertake. Creating an environment that kids can get excited about, however, doesn't have to be so involved. During our study of space, Bob, a fellow teacher, and I built two planetariums. We learned about them in a wonderful two-week residential class we took one summer through the Oregon Museum of Science and Industry. The planetarium was extremely easy to make. It required about twenty feet of heavy-duty agricultural plastic. We folded the plastic in half and taped the sides with heavy duct tape. Next, we had to cut out opposite corners. In one corner, we taped a box fan to the plastic (the air flowing inward). When the fan was plugged in, the plastic expanded, and the whole class, who carefully crawled in through the other hole, was able to fit inside. Once inside, they poked holes through the plastic to make the constellations. We had to play around with the size of the holes using available light; we started out with pins and ended up with one of those long knife sharpeners.

The kids did research on constellations and put on star shows for other classes in our school and for another school in our district. We were also asked to give the show to a science fair at a private school in the area. I could only take three kids with me, but it was a great experience for those three.

The planetarium could not, of course, stay up all the time, which was another reason flexibility was so important. The planetarium took up most of the middle part of the room, and when we put on shows, we needed to be able to move tables and shelves easily. We also covered the walls in black roll paper so it felt as if we were in space, and mounted the children's research and projects on the walls around the room.

Forest

Last year, when we were studying forests, we decided to turn the room into a forest, an easy transformation that didn't call for much rearrangement of furniture.

We were talking about evergreen and deciduous trees when we had the idea. The kids chose groups for the tree they would make. Each group came up with a plan for a tree and each was given a carpet roll tube (the same as for the island palm trees). We taped these trees to the floor and supported them at the top with string tied to the lights.

The branches of the deciduous trees extended from the carpet tubes to the lights. It was really beautiful. I remember the afternoon we had completed all of the trees. "Let's sit under the trees and tell stories," someone suggested. We sat under the trees telling stories with the lights out. I really felt as if I were in the woods at night. What's more, the kids felt it too.

"I wonder what it would sound like in the woods at night."

"I've camped, I know. You hear raccoons and stuff."

"Oh, let's camp out here! We could bring our sleeping bags!"

"Yeah, cool! But you don't hear raccoons, you hear wolves and foxes."

"I've heard owls."

"We should make owls for our trees."

"Yeah, and other birds."

"What about some other animals too?"

From their questions came ideas and new information to explore, and out of those questions and ideas, I wrote the Forest Design Problem (see Figure 4).

FOREST DESIGN

You need to design a forest.
Your forest needs to have an area of over 200 and under 400 square units. (You may pick your own size of unit.)
Your forest must include the following:

THE TREES

- twice as many evergreen trees as deciduous trees.
- 2/3 of the evergreens must be 2 inches taller than the deciduous trees BUT not over 6 inches tall.
- the other 1/3 of the evergreens must be new growth and smaller than the deciduous trees.
- 2/3 of the evergreens must be conifers.

THE FOREST

- a stream that is at least 24 inches long, but not in a straight line.
- 2/3 of the trees need to have animals in them.

AND...

You will need to label all trees NEATLY.
You will need to write down the area and the perimeter of your forest.
You will need to write down how tall the trees are.
You will need to name your forest.
You will need to write a fiction or non-fiction piece about your   forest.

REMEMBER...BE ORGANIZED!!
AND HAVE FUN!!

FIGURE 4 The Forest Design Problem.

Many times what we do in class comes from what we are actually building, talking about, or wondering about. Many of the projects I make up are based on situations like this. (I don't write them over the summer, hoping they might fit in somewhere during the year.)

"I think we should have a pond in here, Jill, don't you?" asked Zack one afternoon, as we were watching our tadpoles slowly transforming into frogs.

"That would be so cool, Zack! How could we do it?"

"How about just making one out of paper?"

"Yeah. Hey, let's tip a round table over and put the paper around that. How does that sound?"

POND DESIGN

You need to design a pond.
Your pond needs to have an area of 400 square units.
Your pond does not need to be in the shape of a square.
Your pond must include the following items:

>   rocks
>   plants
>   grass around pond
>   tadpoles
>   tadpoles with back legs forming
>   frogs
>   salamanders
>   5 different kinds of pond insects

You must label all items NEATLY.
You will need to figure out the perimeter of your pond.
You need to name your pond.
You will need to write a fiction or non-fiction piece about your pond.

AND...

You need to have 2 times as many tadpoles as frogs.
You need to have 4 times as many insects as salamanders.
You need to put plants in 1/4 of the pond.
You will need to outline the border of the pond in black.
You will need to color in the water.
You will need to cut out and paste on 1/2 of what you make.
You will need to color 1/2 of what you make.

FIGURE 5 The Pond Problem.

"Great! Let's do it." And we did. Many other children came to help make that pond. Rachel thought of putting clear plastic wrap over the top so we could look through it and see the animals and plants in the pond. The kids made paper salamanders, tadpoles, frogs, and pond plants. A few kids took some concrete blocks I use for shelves, put the brown-paper-covered shelves on top, then put them on either side of the pond. These were supposed to be log benches so we could sit in front of the pond. Inspired by that little pond in the middle of the room, I wrote the pond problem (see Figure 5).

I decided to bring the forest sounds the kids wondered about into the room. I bought a tape and played it in the background. The kids were used to hearing music in the room, but this was a bit different and it just added to the overall environment.

Music

I play music all day long on a small tape/CD boom box. I have gathered a collection of tapes and CDs ranging from New Age relaxation to Ella Fitzgerald and Louis Armstrong to Bach. I notice a calmness in the room when the music is on. We know when the music has ended because the noise level begins to rise. Visiting teachers have commented on the music and have later told me that they too began playing music during the day in their own classrooms.

The children's favorites are Bach, Mozart, Ella and Louis, Kenny G, Piano II, Bulgarian chanting, African drumming, and Will Ackerman. The older kids are able to change the CDs and tapes independently when the music ends.

The nice thing too is that the kids know which type of music is good for certain times. During Writing Workshop, they seem to like more classical music. During Reading Workshop, they want quieter New Age relaxation music. And during project times they want "boppy" music (as they call it). Kenny G, or a tape I made consisting of various artists, is a popular choice.

The music is playing when the kids come in the morning, and I don't turn it off until I leave at the end of the day. The kids who have been students in my classroom expect to hear music from the very first day of school.

BEGINNING THE YEAR

When the children come through the door in September, the music is playing but the walls are bare. I leave them that way on purpose. I don't put up colorful butcher paper or an alphabet chart. I need the kids' help in creating our environment, so I couldn't possibly put things up before they arrive. I usually send a note to the parents of new children in August. Walking into a bare first-grade room is a bit of a shock to some parents, and I want them to understand why the room looks the way it does.

Most of the walls in the classroom change constantly. I do start out the year by having a calendar time; I have some wonderful calendar ideas I have collected over the years as well as some of my own. But, come February, I am often bored with it, and I notice that the kids are too. And by that time, we need the valuable wall space, so we usually drop it. I always feel guilty, but I do it anyway. This year, we needed the wall for a project the kids had done, and I felt that the project was more important. Allyn Snider suggested using a movable board for the calendar, but space is such an issue, I'd have nowhere to push it to. I know the calendar is important, but I haven't figured out a way to include it throughout the entire year.

Over the year, the classroom walls reflect what we are studying. This year they were filled with island projects, island problems, island poems and writing, and island art. Although not everything we do is about the island, I usually like to put up those things that are related to our current project.

Another reason the room is bare is that I have no idea what we'll be studying until I see the kids all together. I didn't plan the island project ahead of time, I planned it as we went along. I didn't know we would focus on the island for the entire year. It just happened. It was the way this particular class seemed to want to go.

I love the fact that these children are able to see beyond boundaries. Nothing is impossible, nothing is too much for their imaginations. But we don't see our classroom as a boundary either. We try to get outdoors as often as the Oregon climate will allow and to use resources within the building as well.

BEYOND THE CLASSROOM

I try to bring the curriculum outside for a variety of reasons. In the spring, the children do Quiet Writing. This is something I began when I taught in England. It's similar to Writing Workshop in that the kids can write whatever they want, but they can't talk to each other. Quiet Writing compliments Writing Workshop in that the kids know they have the chance to confer during the day (see Chapter 4). They wouldn't be able to concentrate as they do during Quiet Writing if I didn't give them that chance to talk during Writing Workshop.

For Quiet Writing we go outside, find a spot under the trees away from everyone else, and write. I love Quiet Writing because I also get a chance to concentrate on my own writing. I know it's important for teachers to show their kids that they write, but it's difficult for me to do that during Writing Workshop. I want to have conferences and see what the kids are doing. So it's fun for me to write and share my writing at Quiet Writing. The kids love Quiet Writing because they can concentrate without any distractions. I have seen the level of what they can do soar during this time. I'm not sure why we only do it outside in the spring, but that's the way the kids like it. We've tried it indoors but it just doesn't have the same effect.

Some parts of our curriculum make most sense outside, for example, the Garden Problem (see Chapter 5). When I want the kids to really experience square footage, we need to go outside into the fields. We plotted out one of the gardens to see the actual size; they could only do it outside.

We also do minpins parks outside. I read Roald Dahl's *The MinPins,* in which tiny people called minpins live in the branches of trees, to the kids last year. When we were studying the forest, the children would often pretend that there were minpins in the trees, so I decided to take their interest and curiosity outside. At the side of our school are huge Douglas fir trees, and we went out and sat under them. I made up a story about the minpins wanting to come out of the trees and play on a playground or in a park. The kids needed to make a park for the minpins using only what they could find outside (see insert page 4).

The parks they produced were great! We tried the project again at the beginning and end of this year. The last time we made minpins parks, in June, I decided to have the kids work in pairs, and I added some requirements. Since we were doing a lot with *area* and *perimeter,* I told the partners that their park needed to be at least thirty square units, and that they would need to measure the perimeter. They used an inch as the square unit measurement, and when the park was completed, I asked them to figure out how many square feet it was and to compare these measurements.

The parks were incredible. Some of the kids wanted ponds, so they began figuring out how to make the water stay in the hole they dug.

"Can we use a plastic tub, Jill?" asked Tessia.

"No way, you can only use things outside," I answered.

"Hey Jill!" Carly shouted, "Grant and I want to go and get stones from the play structure. We think we can make the water stay in with stones." That idea inspired many other options. Megan and Alissa found a piece of plastic outside and used that to line their pond. They said they could use it because it was outside when they found it. I wasn't going to argue with that logic, but we did talk about what was a natural material and what wasn't.

Going outdoors is a great way to get beyond the classroom walls, but there are places in the school that help with this as well. Our school librarian runs the library exactly the way I always wished a school library could be run. She lets the kids go to the library when they need to go. I don't have to sign up for a thirty-minute story time; after all, I read to my kids in our classroom. The kids should be able to use the library when they need it: to do research, to work quietly, to use an available computer, or just to check out books. What better way for a child to learn how to use a real library than to *really* use the school library! If the library rules change, it will cause problems for us, but we are used to running into problems and dealing with them head on.

PROBLEMS

Having an African village and a forest of carpet roll tubes can cause some serious problems, not only with the janitor but with the district fire marshall. I have had numerous battles with the fire marshall over the last three years, but I have learned to work with him instead of fighting him. (One fight almost shut our school down. It was pretty bad, but I did end up doing what he said.) He will always win; I just need to know that before getting into arguments with him. It seems that butcher paper cannot be put up in long strips on the walls. That was difficult. The walls in my classroom are so ugly, I have used butcher paper to cover them. But the fire marshall would not permit this. Instead of feeling defeated, I use the flame-resistant crepe paper I found in our school's supply room. It must be about fifty years old but it does the job.

I have learned to call the fire marshall and discuss things with him before I build. I knew the hills and mountain structure would make him faint, so I called to explain it to him beforehand. He suggested putting baking soda in with the papier-mâché. That was easy. He also suggested that I spray the entire structure with fire-resistant spray. (He said that our school maintenance person put a gallon at every school.) I found it, sprayed the hills and mountain structure after the kids had left, and that was that. Much easier than a fight.

I have also learned to work with the school janitor. I asked him not to sweep or vacuum during the whole time we had the African village up. That seemed to calm him down when he stepped into the room.

The other physical problem we run into is that of space. Because much of what we do in my classroom is in project form, space is crucial. I can never find enough room for all of the boxes and the "junk" we need for these projects, and while they are being created, there is never any good place to put them. In my first year, a parent built me two tables for storage. They have been very useful—but I still need more room. They just didn't design classrooms forty years ago for the way I teach today, and that's very frustrating. I can't say I've solved it yet.

Another big frustration is the shortage of supplies. Even when budget cuts weren't an issue, I still found it hard to keep a good supply of pencils and paper. When I stopped to figure out why, I decided that since we don't use worksheets, workbooks, or textbooks, paper is in high demand. I hate asking the kids to bring in supplies, and I rarely do, so I have used the money allocated to me for textbooks to buy supplies. But even if I had no problems with the fire marshall or the janitor, and had an abundance of supplies, the biggest problem in our room would still be the mess.

Our classroom is a mess 95 percent of the year. It's hard to avoid it. Learning and creating are messy. One reason I like building huge structures is to obscure the mess!

The kids know that the classroom is theirs, but that means that the mess is theirs as well. Every once in a while, we all get sick of the clutter and do a major overhaul, but I don't think the mess and clutter take away from what and how the kids are learning. On the contrary: one step into the room and it is apparent that exciting and important things are happening. Any child in the room is able to explain what is going on and what project is what.

One reason the room is so cluttered is that I save everything. I don't send a thing home during the year. The kids' work stays in their portfolios for the entire year.

I used to blame the mess on myself. I thought that my room just reflected that I was an untidy person. I don't think that way anymore. I would hate to have a perfectly clean, totally uncluttered room. I need to see learning in progress. I need to see that things are happening. If I thought the clutter—the projects, art work, work-in-progress, and supplies—was getting in the way of learning, I would restructure the room. But in actual fact, I see more learning going on because of it.

The kids know that it is their responsibility to clean the room. Like all of us, sometimes they slack off in their duties. But for the most part, when I say "clean," they clean. They know that if they don't, they won't be able to do any more projects. They know that if I find a paintbrush in the sink, I'll take the paints away.

I have learned to use the limitations of our classroom environment in a way that is conducive to my philosophy of teaching. If I had my own way, I'd redesign the entire school. I'd want windows running the entire length of the room, I'd want nice furniture and no Formica, I'd want an art space . . . . But, since I can't have those things, I'm doing my best to get as close to that ideal as I can.

4

There Are No Recipes:

A "Typical" Week

A typical week? I don't think there is such a thing in my classroom, but there are typical activities that are scheduled at regular times throughout the week. Writing Workshop, Reading Workshop, Math Workshop, Art Workshop, and project times are extremely important, and I try to make sure we fit them in. But flexibility is also important. If the children are involved in a major project and we can't stick to our regular schedule one day, I don't panic. The day's work is so integrated, I never worry that I am neglecting something, yet even then, I wouldn't give up Writing or Reading Workshop for anything.

I used to hold Reading and Writing Workshops in the morning, but now I've moved them to the afternoon. I find that I like the quiet afternoons better, and the kids seem to like them too. We usually start the day doing projects, like the jobs the kids worked on during our island study. I try to finish the day doing what we were doing in the morning. It's a nice daily closure, and for clean-up purposes, it's a big help. The kids can leave what they are doing on the tables knowing that when they walk into the room the next morning, they will be able to get right back to work. This doesn't always happen—it depends on the project—but this system has worked very well when we are in the middle of something big, like creating the island. In the morning, we usually have Math Workshop and/or time to work on the problems I've given the kids, and this sometimes spills over into the afternoon. I run the Art Workshop much like the one described by Karen Ernst in her book, *Picturing Learning.* I highly recommend it to anyone interested in organizing an Artist's Workshop. There are also two specials the kids go to throughout the week, physical education and music. So, although a typical week is never really typical, I will describe the workshops and projects and how choice, challenge, and independence are constantly reinforced for the children.

WRITING WORKSHOP

When I initially picked up Nancie Atwell's *In the Middle* and realized it was for middle school teachers, I wondered how it could possibly help me with six-year-olds. But it turned out to be more helpful than any other educational book I have read. It confirmed and validated everything I believe in about writing with children. Since that first experience, I have run Reading and Writing Workshops in my classroom every year and doubt that I will ever give them up. I have thanked Nancie Atwell in person and in writing, but I feel I need to thank her for being confident enough to go out on a limb and do what she thought, what she truly believed, with how children learn. I have felt out on a limb often throughout my teaching career, and I only have to think of her to remember I am sticking to my philosophy. I am doing what I truly believe with how children learn. So—thanks again, Nancie!

The Writing Workshop is run mainly by the kids. They keep two files: one for their work-in-progress and the other for their drafts (this is their writing portfolio). From the first day of school, they know that in Writing Workshop they can write whatever they want. They draft, edit, conference, revise, and publish. I have found that my practice differs from other writing workshops I've seen in that I only publish pieces that have been edited and/or revised. Some teachers "publish" pieces in the child's invented spelling, but I disagree with this because the piece is an early draft. In the real world, editors clean up our writing before it is published. I believe children need to learn the difference between a final copy and a published piece. If I ask a child to do a final copy, she edits her draft, has a conference with a peer and with me, and redoes her piece in pen or on the computer. If a child wants his piece published, I will type up the edited piece in conventional spelling.

Spelling

Spelling: what a major controversy. I finally feel comfortable with my philosophy about spelling, but I am often challenged by other teachers because I don't give weekly spelling tests. "How can you *not* do it?" they ask. How *can* I? How can I give the same test to a class whose ages span four years? Even without the four-year age span, how could I give the same spelling words to a class of children of the same age? Children, especially young children, acquire written language at such different rates, it seems unreasonable to ask them to participate in the same weekly spelling test. I am often questioned about my "spelling program," and I say that my spelling program is getting the kids *writing*. They write constantly, all day long. Their progress shows in their daily work. Why would I ask them to waste their time memorizing lists of words when they most likely wouldn't transfer what they've memorized to their drafts? I really like Sandra Wilde's book, *You Kan Red This*. She gives examples and cites research explaining why so many spelling programs are inappropriate for the majority of the class.

During conferences, I assist the children with spelling *strategies*. Memorizing lists of words doesn't help them learn the strategies they need to spell unfamiliar words, and if children don't have ways of approaching spelling, then weekly spelling tests are that much more useless.

In a conference, Rachel showed me one of her favorite strategies.

"I know this is spelled wrong," she said, pointing to *cot*, her spelling of the word *coat*.

"Yes, it is. How do you think it should be spelled?"

"Well, let me do this," and she proceeded to make a list of possibilities. She wrote:

cote
coet
coat
coet
coit

"I think it's this one," she said, circling *coat*. This list demonstrated several things about Rachel's strategy. She knew enough about the long vowel sound /o/ to include all these possibilities. Her approach to spelling is visual. She recognized the correct spelling of the word *coat* when she saw it. If Rachel had circled *coet*, I might have asked her to look again to see if she could figure out why that wasn't the right choice. I wouldn't have questioned Chris that way. If he had circled *coet* after making a list like Rachel's, I would have been content to see how much he knew about long vowel patterns. Clearly Chris and Rachel are at very different points in their spelling progress. Knowing the children individually guides me in determining when and what to ask of them.

Many of the other kids also use Rachel's strategy. They learn it from me or from watching other children. But it is not an effective approach for everyone. JB, for instance, needs to be able to draft quickly and then go back and fix his spelling mistakes. He is very able to do this by sight. Josh, on the other hand, a very capable speller, uses a dictionary to help him spell difficult words. And Joshua uses a combination of these two strategies. The best drafting strategy is writing down what you hear in a word. When I need to spell an unfamiliar word, I write down the sounds I hear in the word. Then, if I am using the computer, I can spell-check it; if not, I'll look it up in the dictionary. I often try the listing strategy in my head (adults do this all the time; we just don't think about it when we're doing it).

All these strategies are useful and valid. Children who use such strategies know that there are more ways to spell than by just memorizing words. But some children aren't ready for specific strategies. They need to continue experimenting with invented spellings.

Megan would have stopped writing if she had been asked to memorize the spelling of words. Her confidence would have been shot. When she began the year, she only wrote words she could spell: *cat, hat, mat* . . . it was awful! I was sorry that she wouldn't take any risks. But as time went on, and I questioned her about her pieces, she began to try to draw on what she knew about sounds. She was bright enough to be shown different strategies, but she was not yet confident enough to accept these kinds of suggestions. Over the year, as she became more confident, I was able to ask her to look over her drafts and see if she could add or take away sounds from the words she had written (see Figure 6).

The major reason I don't use weekly spelling tests or focus the children's writing on spelling is that I want them to leave my class as *writers*. It's more

FIGURE 6   An example of Megan's early writing.

important to me to have a class full of writers who fill a page with exciting leads, dialogue, description, characters, and voice, than to have a class that is only able to spell. What good are perfectly spelled words if a child can't write?

Leads

We work on leads, voice, description, dialogue, and character development constantly. I sometimes pull kids aside for a mini-lesson, but I usually have discussions during conferences. These discussions are overheard by others and children pick up on them. One day I was having a talk with Dave about leads.

"David, this lead is great!"

"What's a lead?"

"Oh, a lead is what grabs the audience. It is what makes the reader want to keep on reading. You have a wonderful way of doing this." Here is what David wrote:

Long long ago when tall masts of ships filled the harbors and the sea rocked below them, there was a boy named William. He loved watching the ships go in and out of the harbor and the strong sailors unfurl the sails. But most of all, he wanted to be a sailor.

The next day, Laura ran up to me and said, "Jill, listen to this lead!"

Hi there! My name is Rashelle the raccoon. I'm here to tell you about a horrible part of my life. You see, one black misty night I was walking down a steep, rockey hill, when I spotted a bunch of goldish colored lights.

After that, during question and comment time—the time the children share their writing—they began commenting on the leads of the pieces. How wonderful to hear a six-year-old talking about a lead! Many of the kids started to revise their leads. I am often asked about editing and revising. They are frequently clumped together as one process, but they are actually quite different. Editing focuses mainly on mechanics. Revising, in contrast, is changing a piece of writing so that it makes more sense, includes more description, opens with an exciting lead, is written in a clear voice, or has a good conclusion.

Revision

Over the years, I have learned how inexperienced writers see revision. Usually, when the youngest children in my class revise, they rewrite the same story again and again. This is what Alissa did for an entire year when she was a first grader. She would begin each story with "One day a little girl went to the park." Instead of going on to add more to sentences, she would begin the story again: "One day a little girl named Alissa went to the park."

Children will revise their writing so that it makes sense to their audience. This often occurs when they share questions and comments. Children read their piece, and if it is clear that it makes no sense to the audience, their comments will confirm their lack of understanding: "I don't get it" or "What were their names?" are common remarks. At this point, the writer will usually go back and revise the piece in response to these questions and comments. Most writers *want* others to understand what they have written, and when they are aware of the need, they can add names or clarify.

Alissa wanted the rest of the class to be interested in her story, so, after sharing her piece and responding to questions and comments, she added to it.

As these young writers become more experienced, I encourage them to revise, often during individual conferences, by asking, "Does this make sense?" If the answer is "no" then I ask them how it can be changed to make sense. Although there is no formula for conference questions, I often find myself asking

Does this make sense?
Who are you talking about?
What else could you add to this?
Does this ending fit the rest of the story?
Is this lead exciting?

When a child goes back to make changes in a piece, she is revising. More experienced writers are able to revise their drafts for clarity and to add description, strong leads, and conclusions (see Figure 7).

Editing

Editing for inexperienced writers means looking closely at the mechanics of what they have written. They will check over words they think are misspelled by adding or taking away sounds. As they become more experienced, they not only edit for spelling, they look for places where punctuation is needed and try to determine if the sentence sounds right grammatically. Children learn how important mechanics are in helping the reader understand what they have written. For instance, when Dave was filling pages with complex dialogue, it was impossible for him or his readers to know who was talking until, during a conference, I asked him, "Wait, who's talking now?" This was a perfect moment for me to show him that writers use quotation marks to distinguish between different speakers.

Both revision and editing are important, yet they are very different processes. Like all writers, children need to revise and edit their drafts so that their meaning is clear and is expressed the way they intended. When they have completed a draft and want to revise, edit, and publish, they get a revision and editing check sheet. I put these together so the kids could keep track of what they have worked on, and so I know that they have attended to any problems in the piece. The revision check sheet asks:

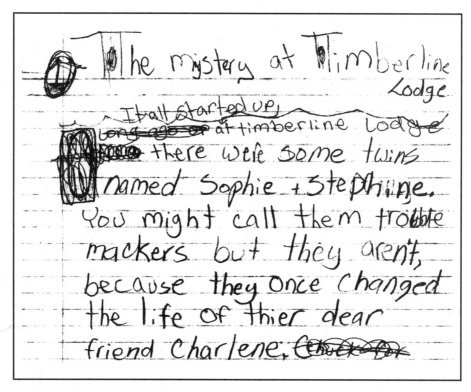

FIGURE 7 Drafting and revising for a good lead.

Does the piece make sense?
Did you describe the characters?
Did you describe the setting?
Is it written in your voice?
Is the lead strong?
Is the conclusion strong?
Have you said everything you want to say?
Did you read this to someone else?
Are you ready to edit?

The editing check sheet asks:

Did you check your spelling? How?
Did you add periods?

Did you use capital letters at the beginning of sentences?
Did you put in quotation marks?
Did you edit with someone else?
Are you going to publish this?
Why should it be published?

I rarely encourage inexperienced writers to rewrite their piece from scratch. If a child is publishing a piece, there is no reason to rewrite it neatly because it will be typed. And if kids are constantly asked to rewrite their work before publishing, they soon lose interest. What writer in the real world sends a manuscript to a publisher that doesn't require an editor? (See Figure 8.)

During Writing Workshop, children are drafting, editing, revising, illustrating, conferring, and collaborating, as I save a big chunk of the day for these activities. Writing Workshop usually lasts for an hour and fifteen minutes, sometimes a bit more, sometimes a bit less. We try to include time for sharing drafts and for questions or comments. The children love sharing their drafts. Not only do they get to practice reading in front of an audience, but they also get ideas during this sharing time.

Writing Workshop is a wonderful way for children to begin to experience choice, challenge, and independence. Kyle demonstrated both independence and challenge when he wrote the following sentence: "I did not ⌣ yes you did ⌣ ." When I asked him what the lines meant, he explained, "Oh, you know how you talk and the air comes out of your mouth? Well, those lines are supposed to show the air coming out of their mouths." It was clear that Kyle was experimenting with dialogue. I don't think he was quite ready to learn the proper use of quotation marks, nor did it matter to him. What was important was his confidence and independence in trying this new system.

Choice

A question I hear frequently from teachers who want to begin a Writing Workshop is: "I have kids who won't write. They sit and sit and just draw. What should I do?" My answer: "Just let them—for now." Most kids, especially young ones, need to draw before they write. Some of them are testing out the freedom and the choice given to them during Writing Workshop, and I let them experiment. What I have found is that when other kids are writing, and sharing their writing, and sharing published books, the kids who wouldn't

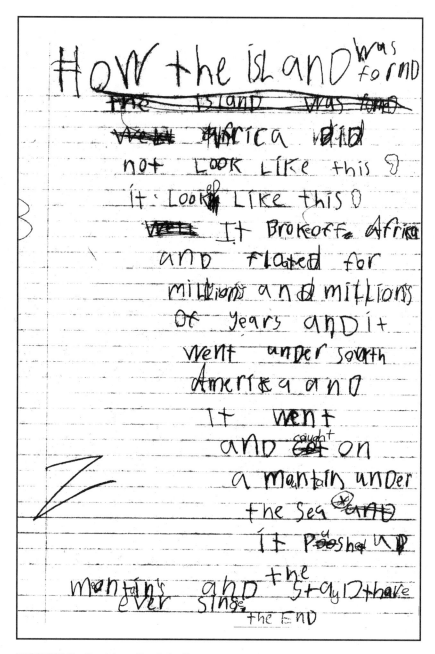

FIGURE 8   Zack's edited draft.

write will begin to. But if a child puts off writing for months, I will be a bit firmer with that child about putting down some writing. It depends on the situation and the child. One year some of the older kids became very interested in making picture books. This went on for weeks and it did make me nervous, until I stepped back and watched how engaged they were.

Many of the kids I am told won't write may not in fact be experiencing a true Writing Workshop. Perhaps they have been assigned a topic to write about or a type of poem to write. Children really need freedom and choice during the workshop time in order to be open to trying other genres, and the more writing, the more experimenting. We all have days when we're stuck. That's what being a writer is all about. That's not to say I wouldn't give children strategies for finding a topic, but they need to experience, as all writers do, the struggle to find the right topic.

I don't do "units" on writing. I don't have poetry week or descriptive writing month. We experience writing as it unfolds. When Dave was writing yet another piece on the Civil War, his lead was so beautiful and so powerful, I suggested that he might want to leave it as a poem instead of expanding it into a whole story.

"Okay, that might work," he said, a bit apprehensively. But he went off to write Civil War poems that were quite incredible (see Figure 9).

> Black men in chains
> Rebel masters yelling
>   and whipping
> Rebel women watching
>   in terror
>   screaming, yelling
> All horrible.
>
> Horse stamping
> Sun rising
> Heart broken rebels
> Tattered flag being
>   rolled up
> War over
> Peace.
>   DAVID

Being able to make choices during Writing Workshop is extremely important. Dave chose to continue writing poems, and because of his interest, other

FIGURE 9 David's accompanying painting for his poem "Black Men in Chains."

children decided to write poems as well. Dave is a Civil War buff and chooses to write 99 percent of his pieces about it. Children should be encouraged to write about what interests them. And what interests them usually interests their audience—the other children in the class. Many of the children write about wars and planes and ships. During the question and comment time it is apparent that the rest of the class is interested in this topic.

Rachel and Laura went through a phase in which they wrote only spooky stories. The class loved them, so they kept doing it. Children know who their audience is and it is rarely an audience of adults. Many teachers I have talked to say they get upset because their kids write about the same topic day in and day out. But if they stopped to think about the audience those children are writing for, I bet they'd understand the kids' interest a bit more.

Because most of the time the children are allowed to choose what they write about, and because they know their audience, it is easier to ask them occasionally to write about a specific topic or to write for a different audience. They can write letters, poems, pieces about books they have read, notes, explanations of mathematical strategies, records of scientific observations and research, for example, and for other audiences because they have been given the opportunity to practice writing freely. Because I allow them this free choice during the workshop, they are able to accept specific writing projects or assignments. I also believe this is true of reading. If children are given choices about what they read, they are more open to other suggestions.

READING WORKSHOP

The children in my classroom choose books independently from the first day of school. "But what about your first graders who can't read?" some ask. First of all, I believe that *all* my children can read. Second, if I begin choosing for them, how will they learn on their own?

I really do believe all children can read. I'm not talking about words on a page. They can read facial expressions, they can read pictures, they can interpret what interests them. Because I start my thinking at this point, it is easy for me to see the tremendous progress each child makes.

Choice

Most of the youngest, least experienced readers in my class will choose the same books day after day. Do I worry about that? I used to, until I began to look at why they did this. As I discovered, the more familiar a child is with a book, the more confidence that child will have in reading the book. And the more confidence a child has, the more risks she will take with reading. The need to take risks is central to my philosophy of learning to read.

Grant began with me as a first grader. He couldn't read many words yet, but he would choose only long novels to read, and I let him do this for about a month. He wanted to read so badly, I didn't want to discourage him by telling him he couldn't read those books. Gradually, he began to choose more appropriate books. I helped, but very subtly. During conferences, I would question him about the book. When it was apparent that he didn't know what he was talking about, I would always say, "Are you sure this is a good choice for you?" And one day, about a month later, he finally said no. It was at that point that I knew he was ready to begin to choose more appropriate reading material.

Had I been choosing books for Grant that month, what would he have learned? To read a month earlier? Possibly, but I wasn't concerned about "when" he began to read. I cared that he was able to see where he was in his reading independently. What I wanted to see was whether he was able to choose his own books.

Progress in reading is not just learning to read words on a piece of paper. I look to see if the child can choose appropriate material, what strategies the child has learned for reading unfamiliar words, and how the child retells what he has read. These all occur during Reading Workshop time (see Figure 10).

My Reading Workshop is also based on Nancie Atwell's *In the Middle*, in that children choose their own reading material. We have sharing times and conferences, as well as times when they can work on projects related to the books they have read. Many times a child will choose the same book as a friend and they will read the book together.

Literature Groups

After whole language became "big," and many teachers phased basals out of the curriculum, Literature Groups became popular. If done right, Literature Groups can be helpful, but they can also be a way of basalizing children's literature. Putting children into ability groups, having them sit in a circle and take turns reading aloud, and giving them vocabulary and questions to answer about a work of children's literature are practices not much different from using a basal. Children need to read, they need to retell, they need to learn how to learn new words as they read; but most important, they need to be able to choose.

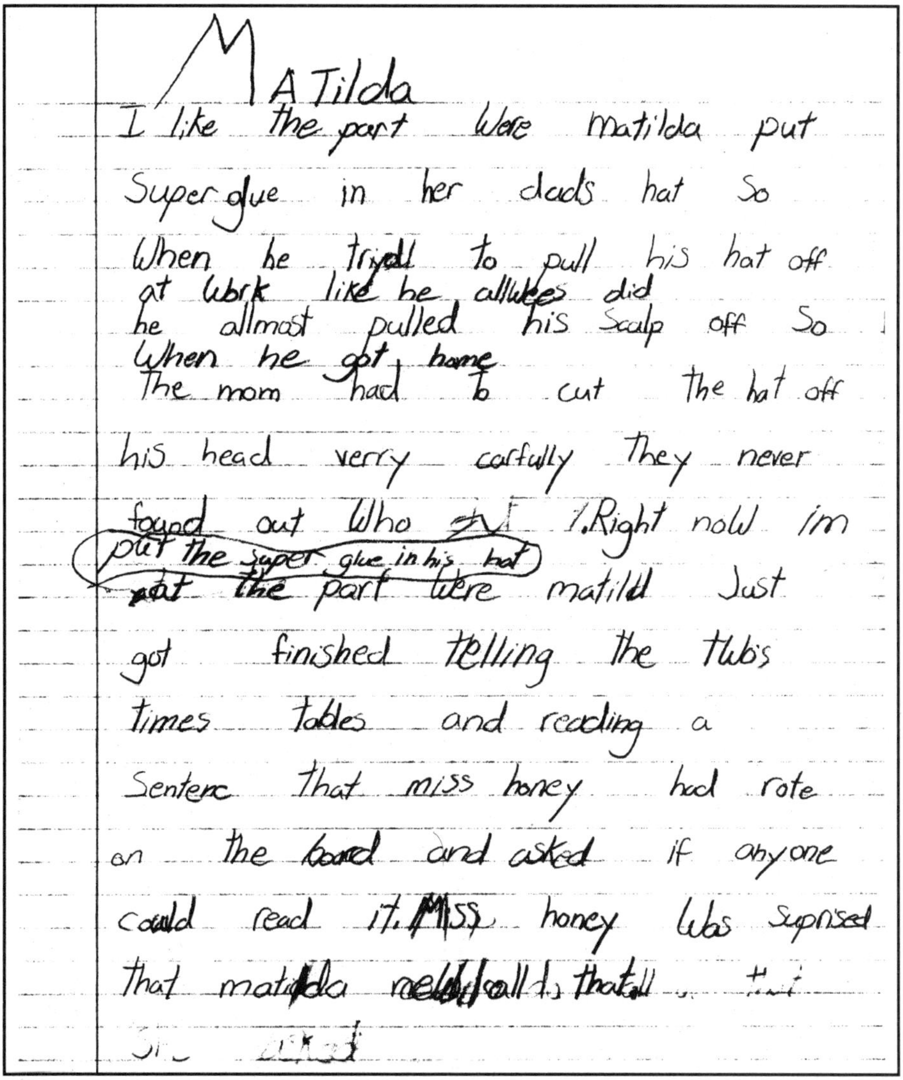

MATilda

I like the part were matilda put Super glue in her dads hat So When he tryd to pull his hat off at work like he alluves did he allmost pulled his Scalp off So When he got home The mom had to cut the hat off his head verry carfully They never found out who ~~that~~. Right now I'm ~~put the super glue in his hat~~ ~~at the part were~~ matild Just got finished telling the tubs times tables and reading a Sentenc that miss honey had rote on the board and asked if anyone could read it. Miss honey was suprised that matilda ~~neld call to that all~~ + ~~she asked~~

FIGURE 10   Josh's Reading Workshop review on *Matilda.*

Rachel, Carly, and Laura all decided to read Patricia MacLachlan's *Sarah, Plain and Tall* together during the year. They met and set up a schedule for how much they would read, what kinds of projects they would do, and how often they would discuss what they had read. They were forming an independent study group, which was more meaningful to them than an assigned ability group.

That's not to say I don't run similar groups; I do. But I don't put the kids in Literature Groups constantly—maybe once, or twice at most, during the year. So how do the kids learn to read? By reading. By choosing books, by looking at books, by sharing books, by writing books, by experiencing literature, and by constantly responding to questions.

Progress

I don't look at children as "slow" or "below grade-level." These terms have no meaning for me. Rather, I look at children as incredible beings who are able to soak up more information than any other creatures on the planet. If I looked at children as "slow" I'd fall into the trap of comparing them to each other and to someone else's set of norms, which have nothing to do with the child or the class. I am hesitant to refer any of the children to special services like Chapter I or Reading Recovery.

Reading Recovery. I am concerned about this program. I wonder about the name. I don't look at the seven- and eight-year-old children in my class who aren't reading yet as needing to "recover." My problem with reading programs is that they assume all children should be reading at a certain level at a certain age. Instead, I watch for progress in each child. If a child is progressing, I don't see a problem. Even if a child is eight years old and still struggling with *Little Bear,* I don't rush the child off to a reading program. We all progress at different rates when we learn something new. Young readers deserve respect. Certainly, there may be benefits to one-on-one programs like Reading Recovery. But it concerns me that this program is a regimented pull-out program in which the adult sees the child as slow. It angers me that so many children are referred to this program, and I am very cautious about its underlying philosophy. "Catching children up"? "Catching them up" to whom?

There are three third-grade children in my class whom another teacher might possibly have referred to a reading specialty program in first grade. One left third grade reading *James and the Giant Peach.* One left third grade reading *The Hardy Boys.* One left reading *The Lion, the Witch, and the Wardrobe.* What was wrong with these children in first grade? Nothing. What did they need when they were in first grade? Respect and time to develop at their own pace. I have also had third-grade children leave my room just beginning to read *Frog and Toad*. These children aren't "slower" than the other children. They are simply progressing at a different rate. Since I began looking at children as individuals who progress at all different rates, I haven't needed to refer any of them to special programs.

Not all children will leave first grade able to read *Frog and Toad* or even *Little Bear*. That's okay. Yes, some children have serious learning problems, but 99 percent of the children that are referred to special reading programs don't truly need them. A visitor to my class once told me that twelve of the children in her class were "identified" as having learning problems. Twelve? She then said that she has an entire class of "slow" children, that they were all "below grade-level" ("grade-level," another term that unnerves me). If we as teachers look at entire groups of children as slow, we need to rethink how we view children. Is it the children who are slow, or is it the expectations of the school system that are unrealistic?

I also find that those children who are acquiring print slowly more often than not have tough issues at home to deal with; not all, but many. When I'm at a low point or feel extremely stressed out about something, the last place I want to be is in a physics class. For many children, especially those with some of the family and outside pressures children are dealing with today, sitting and trying to learn to put words together into sentences and then into a story is like being in a physics class. We need to look at where children are coming from before we stick labels on them. And for some reason, more often that not children are labeled because of their reading ability.

The children in my class are not arranged according to ability. They know what they can read, what they can choose, and what will be challenging to them. It's easy to know what will challenge a new reader, but even very experienced readers need challenges.

Tessia, a second-grader, read most of C. S. Lewis's books in first grade. She read Roald Dahl, *The Secret Garden,* and this year read the entire Book of Three series and *The Hobbit*. The challenge for her was knowing when to take a break from such intense reading.

During one Reading Workshop, I sat down next to her on the couch and asked her what she was reading.

"Nothing," she said as she hid the book.

"Oh, come on Tessia, what is it? You know I'm interested," I said, even though I already knew what it was.

"Oh, okay. Here," and she showed me *Little Bear*.

"Tessia, I think it's great that you're reading this. You probably never had the chance to read it before because you learned to read so quickly. It's actually a challenge for you to read this, to *know* you need to read it. Good for you!" And she preceded to read the entire Little Bear series. She would even talk about it during book share time. What struck me was that no one even commented on the fact that Tessia was reading *Little Bear.* With so many different books, the kids are more interested in *what* the other kids are reading than in how fat it is or what level someone is reading on. The children's respect for each other's ability is phenomenal, especially considering the age span.

For the incoming first graders, the first few weeks, when they see the older kids reading novels and chapter books, are difficult. Megan was devastated and told her mother she'd never be able to read like the "big kids." I decided that if Megan was feeling like this, others were feeling it too. So I brought the first graders, along with two third graders and two second graders over to the platform for a "pep talk."

"JB, do you remember what it felt like when you first came into the class as a first grader?"

"Yeah, I was kind of scared. And I didn't think I'd ever be able to do anything. But after a few weeks, things got easier. It must be harder for you guys, though, because here we are so much older."

"Anna, you came last year and you were younger than the second graders. How did it feel?"

"Oh, it was weird! But they helped me and it was okay." Our talk went on like that for a long time. It was great hearing what the older kids had to say, but it was more exciting seeing the faces of the new kids begin to relax. They just needed reassurance from kids who had experienced the same anxiety.

Megan soon began to relax and to learn what her own abilities were. When she gained more confidence in herself, she was able to take risks in her reading and it became easier for her. She was even able to begin to take on challenges and to accept advice from others.

Sharing

Reading Workshop lasts from forty-five minutes to an hour depending on whether we do a book share or not. Book shares are just what the name would suggest: those who want to, share what they are reading. This serves a couple of purposes. It is a great way to check if a child can retell what she has read.

And it is a great way for kids to share with each other. Sometimes I gather the kids in groups and have them share together.

For one small group share time, I asked the groups to share their books first. Then they were to think of something that was similar in each of their books and draw these similarities on a big piece of paper. This was a difficult task since the groups were so mixed. One group had kids reading books ranging from *The Dog*, a picture book with limited words, to *The Book of Three*. Their drawings were great and it was fascinating to see what similarities they could come up with.

The children don't do activities like this on a daily, or even a weekly, basis. I want the kids to have most of the Reading Workshop to read and to have conferences with me.

Strategies

During conferences, I will listen to children read and try to learn about what strategies the child is using. I try to discourage most children from sounding out words. What happens when children sound out words is that, by the time they have sounded out the word, they have forgotten what they have read.

I encourage the children to skip words, to try to substitute words, or to keep reading and then go back. By encouraging these strategies, I have smoother and more fluent readers. When I hear children who have been taught to read by learning each phonetic sound sound out words, what I notice is that they stumble over each word trying to "get it," but when asked to explain what they've read, they have no idea. In my room, what we talk about is reading for meaning.

"What's happening in your book Alissa?" I asked during a conference.

"I don't really remember that part."

"Can you tell me anything that happened?"

"Hmm. I don't remember." She was halfway through a book.

"Since you don't remember, what does that tell you about this book?"

"It was too hard."

"Yeah, I think maybe it was, since you don't remember what happened. Was it fun to read?"

"Not really."

"Why do you think you are reading it then?"

"I don't know. I just wanted to try it."

"That's great, Alissa, choosing a challenging book like this, but remember that understanding what you read is most important."

That was an easy conference because the book really was too difficult for Alissa. When she tried to read it to me, she couldn't. What I find frustrating is having children come into my room who have learned to read words but not to read for content or meaning.

Ben, who came to the class as a second grader, began the year reading a Matt Christopher sports book. I sat down next to him to listen to him read, and I was quite impressed with how smoothly he was reading. But when I asked him to retell what he had read, he went blank. He could read words, but he didn't know what he was reading. I asked him to start choosing less challenging books and after each chapter, to come and talk to me about it. This really helped him, and by the end of the year he was able to try Matt Christopher again and understand what he was reading.

Besides conferences and book shares, the kids also write about books they are reading. Some years I use reading journals, other years I periodically have the kids write about a character or a similarity between what they have read and their own life. This kind of writing helps when they are asked to do research or mathematical writing.

MATH WORKSHOP

Not until I began to understand that the acquisition of mathematical concepts is very similar to the acquisition of language, did I feel comfortable with my math program. I used to watch to see when a child could do addition facts to ten, then twenty, then subtraction, and so on. I used to do units on fractions and multiplication. But when I was questioning units on phonetic sounds, I began questioning units on mathematical concepts. Neither is "wrong" nor "harmful," yet neither is very meaningful in terms of internalizing a concept.

Children internalize new concepts—such as letter sounds—when they use them constantly. Teaching a /b/ sound one week and then forgetting about it and not letting children experiment with it in writing isn't very efficient learning. I have found that the same is true for mathematical concepts. Years ago, when I used to teach the fraction unit, we rarely used fractions again until months after the unit had ended. What was I teaching fractions for anyway? What were we doing that we needed fractions? It seemed to contradict my philosophy of learning.

I began to change my approach to math by reminding myself that language and math should be presented to children in the same way. I never officially called our "math time" Math Workshop until a group of teachers I was teaching in a course used the term to describe the program. I have since adopted it.

Skills

I don't do units on a specific skills. Instead, I try to have the kids experience these concepts through projects, problems, mini-lessons, and a choice time. And I don't teach conventional algorithms, the way many of us were taught. An algorithm is any multi-step procedure. The conventional way, the system we all learned for solving problems like 46 + 37, is just one algorithm for solving that problem. I let the children invent their own procedures for solving multi-step problems, and I encourage them to develop strategies for learning math facts, since memorizing facts doesn't allow children to discover strategies on their own. For instance, some children in my class may find the answer to 4 + 5 by knowing that 4 + 4 = 8, and adding 1 more. Others add 5 + 5 and take away 1. It is important for children to be able to experiment and try out their own strategies.

Problem-Solving

Through many long talks with Allyn Snider, I have learned that children need to experiment with numbers, come up with their own algorithms, test those strategies and come up with other methods, and eventually discover the most efficient way for themselves. Sometimes, the most efficient strategy resembles a conventional algorithm; sometimes not. What is easy and efficient to a child may differ from the traditional way we were taught.

Marilyn Burns writes about the importance of having children invent their own algorithms in her book *About Teaching Mathematics*.

> It's important for children to understand that algorithms are procedures that have been invented by people to carry out calculations that are done repeatedly. It's important for them to learn how algorithms are based in the structure and logic of our number system. Also, it's important for children to understand that one particular algorithm may be no better or more efficient than another, and that many methods, including ones they

invent themselves, are equally valid. There is no need for all students to do arithmetic calculations in the same way any more than it is essential for all children to develop identical handwritings or writing styles.

Children need to have the time to figure out solutions to problems independently. They need to know they have choices in how they solve problems. I have unifix cubes, various types of place value units, fraction pieces, pattern blocks, a variety of sizes of graph paper, and an assortment of other manipulatives. The kids know they can use all of these materials in solving problems. They also know that after they have solved a particular problem, I will question them about how they did it.

The kids explain their procedure in writing, in pictures, or both. This is an extremely important step in problem-solving. Their explanations, both oral and written, show me not only if they understood the problem, but how they solved it. Many people have asked, "But what about the youngest children, who can't write yet?" I don't often separate writing in words and writing in pictures when I explain math solutions. Sometimes it is much easier to explain a problem using drawings (see Figures 11a and 11b).

Choice

Because the children learn about choice, challenge, and independence through the problems I make up, they are quick to think up their own games, problems, and activities during choice time in Math Workshop. In Math Workshop children experience not just addition and subtraction, but a wide range of mathematical concepts, including measurement, probability and statistics, geometry, patterning, place value, multiplication, division, fractions, design, and problem-solving, throughout the year.

I often begin Math Workshop with a specific mini-problem. I do this to make sure the children explore all the concepts important to their understanding over the course of the year. It would be foolish for me to believe that I could monitor all of the children's progress in math by doing projects. Through the mini-lessons and these mini-problems, I am confident we touch on all the concepts children need to learn (see Figure 12).

During Math Workshop the kids use the materials in the room to make math games, play math games, work on specific concepts, or do anything else they can

It takes 2 hours to cut down one small palm tree.

How long would it take to cut down 2 small palm trees and 4 large palm trees if the large palm trees are 4 times as big as the small ones?

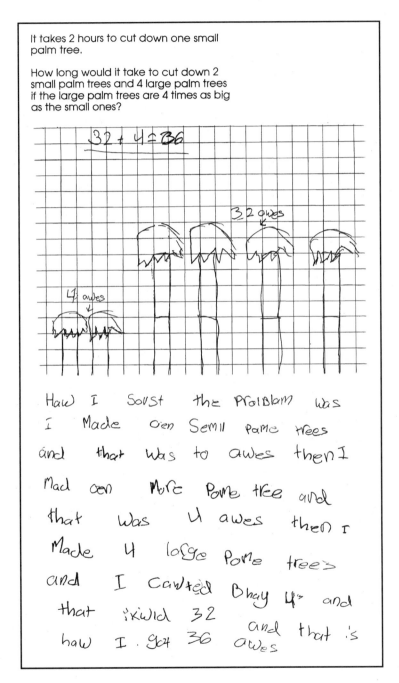

How I Solvst the ProlBlam was I Made oen Semll pame trees and that was to awes then I Mad oen More Pome tree and that was 4 awes then I Made 4 large Pome trees and I Cawtted Bhay 4's and that iKiwld 32 and haw I got 36 awes and that's

FIGURE 11a Morgan uses a drawing to problem-solve.

NECKLACE PROBLEM

Zack found some shells and decided to give them to Rachel. Rachel decided to make a necklace with it. Josh came over with a bunch of pieces of coral. He asked Rachel if she could use them for her necklace. She took them and made the necklace.

The pattern went like this:

shell coral shell coral coral shell coral coral coral...

..it went on and on until there were 12 corals and the last one was a shell.

How many shells were on the necklace? 13

How many pieces of coral were on the necklace? 78

HOW DID YOU SOLVE THIS PROBLEM????

Also...how in the world did Rachel manage to put the shells and coral into a necklace????

i tok A pi's oF GRaF PaPR. AND MaDC sfere FoR CoRal. i Gaot > 8 pesiS oF CoL AND 13 Shels. But Bu FoR i usD GRaF PPR. i usD uNU Fics Cubs But THay WeR ta kiNg to Loll So i usD GRaF PaPR.

BY JosH C.

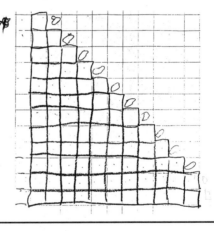

FIGURE 11b   Joshua explains and graphs the Necklace Problem.

think of that involves mathematical concepts. Many children have taken simple games I've made up and expanded them to make them more challenging.

The problems I make up for the kids are based on what we are studying. I don't write these until we are immersed in what we are learning about. The Pond Problem came about from the kids interest in ponds, the Forest Problem from our study of forests. This year I used the animals and land forms of islands as a basis for math problems. (See Chapter 5 for a step-by-step look at the Garden Problem.)

These problems are complex and difficult (they wouldn't be problems if they were easily solved). In the introduction to *Posing and Solving Problems with Storyboxes*, Donna Burk and Allyn Snider state that "a *real* problem is a question for which there is no immediate answer (to the problem-solver). In other

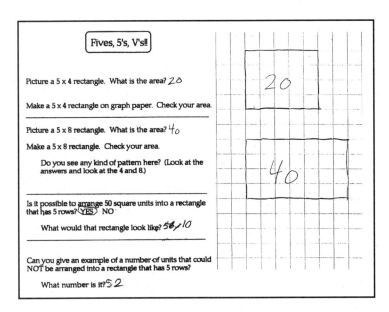

Fives, 5's, V's!!

Picture a 5 x 4 rectangle. What is the area? 20

Make a 5 x 4 rectangle on graph paper. Check your area. _____

Picture a 5 x 8 rectangle. What is the area? 40

Make a 5 x 8 rectangle. Check your area.

    Do you see any kind of pattern here? (Look at the answers and look at the 4 and 8.)

_____

Is it possible to arrange 50 square units into a rectangle that has 5 rows? (YES) NO

    What would that rectangle look like? 5 x 10

_____

Can you give an example of a number of units that could NOT be arranged into a rectangle that has 5 rows?

    What number is it? 52

FIGURE 12 Problem-solving with mini-problems.

words, a *real* problem is something your students don't already know how to do." Children don't need lesson after lesson on multiplication in order to solve problems that rely on that concept. In the problems I write, I want children to experience concepts they may or may not be familiar with already.

I also try to come up with problems that turn into projects. For example, one problem/project was making a gameboard. But not all the projects begin with a problem or have a mathematical emphasis. In our classroom, projects take on a wide range of definitions.

OTHER ACTIVITIES

Literacy Choice and Literacy Choice Challenge

Two years ago, when I wanted the kids to experience more independence, I reserved a chunk of the morning for what I called Literacy Choice.

Literacy Choice involves a variety of possibilities related to literacy. The kids decide how they want to spend the hour. The choices usually include the following:

Writing Workshop
Quiet Reading
Partner Reading
Plays about books
Puppet shows about books

The children choose what to do and they do it! After about forty-five minutes, we get together to share what everyone had done, and sometimes to watch plays and puppet shows.

Exploring literacy in this way broadens children's knowledge of what literacy is: it is more than reading a book or writing a story.

I took this idea a step further with Literacy Choice Challenge. I asked the class to do something that shows what they think a favorite author's childhood was like. That was all the instruction I gave them. The kids went off and got to work.

The activities they came up with were impressive: Chuck created a play, Rachel did a hypercard card stack, Bekka wrote and presented a speech, Joshua constructed a gameboard, and Anna and Alissa wrote and performed a play. Many of the children chose to imagine Roald Dahl's childhood because they were familiar with some of his books, but others imagined the lives of authors from Laura Ingalls Wilder to Matt Christopher.

This year we didn't have Literacy Choice every day or even every week. I scheduled it every so often throughout the year. It wasn't that we were bored with it; we had simply moved on to other ideas.

Independent Learning Day

Independent Learning Day (ILD) began one day when Zack asked me, "Jill, I really want to do Writing Workshop during the morning today. Why do we have to wait until the afternoon?" I knew why I wanted the day organized like that, but I couldn't give him a good answer to why he couldn't write when he wanted to.

I decided to ask the kids how they would like working totally independently for a whole day. They thought it sounded "cool." We listed the work (such as Writing Workshop, reading and then writing about what they had read, doing a problem, signing up for a conference with me, doing an observational drawing, and so on) they were expected to complete by the end of the day on our white board, and I gave each child a Post-it note on which they were to write their name. I asked them to move the Post-it every time they began a new item on the list. They had from 9:00 A.M. to 2:00 P.M. to finish everything.

We did ILD once a week for about a month. We ran into problems with it only because we became busy with other projects. Once in a while we'd have Independent Learning Mornings instead. I varied the activities every time: sometimes I'd have the kids carry folders around with them so they could keep their day's work in it. Sometimes I'd schedule mini-lessons that the kids would have to fit into their day.

Independent Learning Days were possible in late January because the kids had been learning to become independent learners since September. Eventually they were able to plan the days and the activities along with me. They became familiar with the organization of ILD just as they had with Literacy Choices. ILD also helped when we needed to plan for a substitute teacher. The kids planned the day so that when the sub came in, they already knew exactly what was expected of them.

Mini-Classes

Kyle was drawing a picture of a Power Ranger. I knew he was drawing it because he had told me, but I couldn't see the shape of the figure at all.

"Kyle, how are you doing that drawing?" I asked him, a bit amazed.

"With colored pencil," he answered, looking at me a little strangely.

"No, I know what you're using. I want to know where you started drawing. From what part of the body?"

"Oh, I always start from the eye." I remembered watching him draw a dolphin once. The final picture showed a detailed dolphin jumping out of the water with a big wave of water under it. He had begun that drawing too with the eye. Because I don't draw, this was fascinating to me. I had just assumed everyone began by drawing the shell of the body and then adding details.

I wanted the other kids to see how Kyle did this so they would have another option when they were drawing. I asked him if he would give a little workshop one day for kids who were interested.

After Kyle's workshop, other children decided that they too had things they wanted to teach. Now, on Friday we have mini-classes taught by the kids.

Mini-Classes weren't new to us. Other classes in our wing of the school had often organized such classes, but they were taught by the teachers and the parents. Now I am committed to having the children run them. It doesn't require much organization. The mini-classes are from 2:30 to 3:00 on Friday afternoon. On Wednesday or Thursday I simply ask if anyone wants to teach a mini-class. After we list about five classes, the kids sign up for the one they want to be in.

When we first started doing mini-classes, I wrote all the possible choices on a piece of paper and passed it out to the kids. They marked their first, second, and third choice, and I then divided the groups up evenly. We talked a lot about not getting first choices. The children knew that all the classes would be fun, and we rarely had pouting when someone didn't get the one they wanted. Another reason I started having the kids choose their mini-class this way was that, if a class was small, it didn't mean the kids didn't like the child giving it, it was because they were interested in the other classes. After a few months the kids were very accustomed to this and were comfortable having only one or two children when they gave a mini-class.

The content of the classes is totally up to the children. Some may seem extremely silly to adults—such as Carly's class on how to make string beards— but it was very popular with the kids, and after all, we do a lot of plays and the kids often need costumes. Other mini-classes are more serious. Dave often teaches one on the Civil War. Some classes may run several weeks in a row because they are so successful. One of the most popular mini-classes of the year was Zack's offering on how to make a briefcase. He took poster board, folded it, and taped the sides. He showed his students how to make handles for the case and then filled it with paper, a folder, some Post-its, and a pencil. Everyone was so jealous after that mini-class, Zack decided that he would teach it every Friday until everyone had made one (see insert page 5).

JB's older brother, Zack, a fifth grader, came to our room and taught a karate class. He was learning karate and was getting very good at it. I talked to his teacher, and she agreed to let him come for that half hour every Friday. Each class lasted about five weeks, and then a new set of six kids could take it. I'm usually not one for karate or fighting sports, but this changed my mind. Zack taught the kids that karate isn't a fighting sport; it is very serious and takes much concentration. It was wonderful to see the transformation of some of my kids when they used the "hi ya!" kicks at recess. They were learning the art of karate, not just the kicks (see insert page 4).

While the kids are teaching their classes, I usually walk around and watch what's going on. Sometimes I'll sit in on a class. I really wanted to learn how Kyle drew. I was intrigued by Dave's knowledge about the Civil War. Often I just let the kids do what they did best, and I sat back and observed.

At 3:00, the groups know that it is their responsibility to clean up whatever mess they have made. When the room is neat, we take the last ten or fifteen minutes of the day to share what everyone did during mini-classes.

One nice thing about the mini-classes is that all the children have a chance to give one if they want to. There is no pressure to do so, but there is no reluctance either after a few weeks. And it's not only the older children who volunteer, it's anyone who wants to share something he or she thinks is special.

5

Holidays, Journeys, and Gardens: Projects

Writing, Reading, and Math Workshop times are all very important parts of the day. They are the times when children learn new skills while also practicing independence, making choices, and learning to challenge themselves. Yet I don't always see writing, reading, math, and science as separate. I like to create situations that engage the children in a wide variety of experiences and concepts at the same time.

During a project, if someone were to walk into my classroom and ask me, "So what are the kids doing now? Math, writing, reading, science, geography . . . ?" it might be difficult for me to answer because of the nature of what they are working on. They may be reading and doing mathematical operations and geography all at the same time.

This chapter will describe three such projects. For the first one, the Holiday Research, the children researched winter holidays and festivals from around the world and then presented their research to the class. That inspired us to create our own island winter festival. In the Journey Problem, they were asked to take a journey starting from the island and travel to various locations around the world. The Garden Problem was a design project the children worked on in order to create a garden plot on the land each of them owned on the island.

The children were able to approach these challenges because of their experience in the workshops. I try to design challenges and problems that will involve my own curriculum goals while also meeting the guidelines outlined by the school district and the state. Then I combine these goals and guidelines together to come up with a meaningful challenge for the children. Often, the kids come up with the idea and I come up with the plan.

I observe the children's progress and their knowledge of specific skills as they work on these problems and projects, but I also observe their risk-taking, their independence, their cooperation in groups and in partnerships, their willingness to take on challenges, and their organizational strategies (see the learner progress wheels described in Chapter 6).

All three of these problems involve a challenge, offer many choices and require the children to do independent work. This reflects my view that problems should indeed be problems—not something easily solved at a glance. The children invested a lot of time in them: four weeks for the Holiday Research and a little over three weeks each for the Journey Problem and the Garden Problem. Through discussion between partners and large group share times, the kids sought their solutions and encountered frustrations. The projects took them across the disciplines—writing, reading, math, science, and social studies.

THE HOLIDAY RESEARCH

Multicultural education begins with the children: they are all different. If they can respect each other's differences, my hope is that they will respect the differences in those outside the classroom. When I taught in England, I was amazed at the religious atmosphere at Christmas. The British state school where I worked (the equivalent of an American public school) put on a Nativity play for the parents, and pictures of Jesus, Mary, and Joseph were prominently posted around the school. It made me feel uncomfortable, and I tried to ignore it. But what I couldn't ignore were the kids in the school, who represented many different cultures. I wondered how they felt during these Christmas festivities. I decided that when I returned to the States, I would make sure my students learned about many different cultures. Where I currently teach in Oregon, the population is culturally homogeneous. In this kind of situation, I believe even more strongly that all children need to learn about other cultures.

Many schools sponsor a "multicultural" month, but I have a problem with the assumption that learning about another country for a month constitutes multicultural education. I try to introduce children to many cultures and beliefs all through the year.

Research

When December came around during the island year, I wanted to combine learning about other cultures with a holiday celebration. We decided to create our own island holiday that would combine different winter celebrations from around the world. To begin this research project, the children chose a winter festival or holiday. Then they were to find out what they could about it, write a draft, revise and edit the draft, and make a final copy, including a bibliography of their sources. They also were asked to make a small project related to their festival and figure out a way to present their research.

I brought in many books—picture books and reference books—about different parts of the world, different countries, and different religions. I asked the kids to choose some of those books, look through them, and take note of any winter holidays or festivals. We met on the platform for a brainstorming session.

Here is the list we made:

Chanukah	Polish Christmas
Kali	Pongol
Snow Festival	Chinese New Year
Solstice	Bonfire Night
Kwanzaa	Brazilian Christmas
Carnival	Dia De Nuestra Señora De Guadeloupe

The kids signed up for whichever festival they wanted to research. Some worked alone, others with partners and still others in small groups (one group consisted of four kids). I wasn't as concerned about how many children were in each group as I was with making sure they signed up for the holiday they wanted.

The kids spent approximately two weeks collecting information from a variety of sources. The project was open-ended: they were able to organize their research on their own. For some research projects, I make check-off sheets for the kids to use as they go along. Some children need help with organization as they proceed with a large research project. Others do better with more open-ended projects, for which they can do the organizing. I give the children as many different options as I can.

The groups went about their organization quite differently. Anna and Steve were studying the Mexican story of Guadeloupe. They collected most of their information from Anna's father, who wrote down what he knew about the holiday. Anna brought it in to share with Steve. Neither Anna nor Steve could read what Anna's father had written, so I read it aloud to them both, while Anna took notes. Steve couldn't read Anna's notes, so she read them to him, explaining what the story was about. Steve also had difficulty writing what Anna had wanted him to write, so she helped him with each letter. She told him that she would do the final copy all by herself since it was hard for him to use a pen (all this from a girl who has been struggling with reading and writing for the past two years).

Josh, JB, and Sharat all took notes on their own from different books and then put them together in one draft. They took turns writing part of the final copy. Laura, Carly, and Kiersten also took notes on their own, but for the final copy, they decided to use the computer. They took turns typing, and then Laura proofread what they had written before printing it out.

When all the final copies were complete, the kids made a map, or maps, of where their holiday or festival took place and added a cover to their report.

Dioramas

The small projects turned out to be very much alike. Zack and I had found dozens of cardboard box bottoms, the ones that cases of soda cans come on, in the staff room. Each group used two box bottoms to make the festival diorama.

We put all the dioramas and written reports on the platform until we were ready to do the presentations (see insert page 5).

Presentations

We didn't want to simply present our research; we wanted everyone to experience the holidays and festivals we had spent so much time and effort researching. So the kids tried to figure out an activity or a presentation that would involve the class. Then they signed up for presentation time. We could have two a day, one in the morning and one in the afternoon. First they presented their written research and their diorama. After they had taken questions and comments on these, they launched into their activity. Each presentation was completely different. The kids were used to coming up with different ways to present their work, and they came through with very creative, interesting, and complex presentations.

Here are some of the activities:

Bonfire Night (England)

Alan had us all make small "fire sticks" using strips of orange, red, and yellow crepe paper, which we taped onto a little stick. He moved all of the furniture out of the way and put our coffee table on its side in the middle of the room. Around the coffee table he put some chairs and instructed us all to sit in a circle. He taught us a chant about Guy Fawkes, and we all pretended to use our little fire sticks to light the coffee table. Alan had covered the coffee table and chair structure with the extra crepe paper and had put a flashlight inside the coffee table. With the lights out, it was easy for us to imagine a real bonfire.

Pongol (India)

Zack and Kyle studied Pongol. During their research presentation they explained that Pongol is a three-day festival and that we would be doing three different things, one in the morning, one right before lunch, and the last at the end of the day. They turned the back room into a temple, covering the entryway with orange butcher paper to make it look like a door. Inside the back room, they covered the lights with dark (fire retardant) crepe paper so their temple would be darker. On "day 1," we were told to enter the temple very quietly. We went in to celebrate the rain. Zack stood on a chair and said something to us all, in a very serious tone, about why we should be so thankful for the rain. Then we were escorted out of the temple to wait for "day 2."

"Day 2" came and we were once again led into the temple. This time, we were told to think about the sun and why it is so important to us. Again, we were led out of the temple.

On "day 3," we did not enter the temple. Zack and Kyle had cleared the middle of the room.

They explained that on the third day, a bull is decorated and money is put in the bull's horn. The people try to snatch the money out of the bull's horn.

Kyle was the bull. He had made bull horns for his head and a money bag to hang from it. Zack ran around the circle in the middle of room trying to grab the money out of Kyle's horns as he ran from Zack. After he had snatched it, he let other kids try.

Snow Festivals (Canada, Japan, and other Northern Countries)

Jacob, Larry, Chuck, and Joshua had us all make snow sculptures out of dough that Joshua's mom had prepared. They explained that, during the snow festivals, parents give the kids money and the kids give presents, and they showed us pictures of snow sculptures.

Carnival (Brazil)

Carly, Kiersten, and Laura explained that Carnival lasts for a long time, and people go crazy and dance in the streets. They had us make costumes: they showed the girls how to make long skirts and the boys how to make long belts. (I'm still not clear about why the boys needed those long belts!) Laura's idea was to have all of us "go crazy" for five minutes. We talked about it.

"Laura, what do you think would happen if we all went wild for five minutes? Think about how long that is." I asked her.

"Well, maybe Zack wouldn't be able to settle down. Or, maybe it's just too long. How about three minutes?"

"Okay, you time three minutes and let me know if that seems like too much time. Think about what the room might be like for that long." After she had timed three minutes, she came back to me and said, "Jill, I think a minute will be enough time."

After we had all put on our costumes, the girls said we could go crazy for one whole minute, but Laura was very firm: when she turned off the music, everyone was supposed to freeze. The music went on and at first the kids were a bit unsure about acting "crazy," as she had put it. So I started dancing and telling everyone to have fun. Some kids got on the tables and some ran around the room. (It's amazing how long just one minute can be.) When the music stopped, so did the kids.

The Festival Memory Books

These festival and holiday presentations may not have been totally accurate in every detail, but the kids learned that not everyone celebrates Christmas, that many people celebrate Christmas in ways different from ours, and that festivals and holidays celebrate what is important to you.

I wanted the kids to be able to record what they were learning, so I made each child a blank book. After each presentation, they would take their books, write the name of the festival, the names of the children who presented, what the activity was, and what they had learned.

Our Island Festival

When all of the presentations were complete, we turned to making up our own island festival island. Each group picked one thing from their own research to bring to our festival. We also combined the names of all of the festivals we studied and came up with this name: Cavlishacamas Dresla Zekar (Tessia was the only one who could ever remember it!).

On the last day before winter break, we celebrated our island festival. Grant and Dave had made a shrine out of a huge box and called it the HESHE. We were to go to the HESHE whenever we wanted to ask for something. We lit candles because the groups that studied Kwanzaa and Chanukah wanted candles. Our candles were in the shape of numbers, which represented our ages: 6, 7, 8, 9, and 33. Five times during the day we would light our candles: each age group lit theirs together, and we all lit mine. We ate food that would be native to our island and danced for a minute, getting crazy. That was our winter festival, and it was important to all of us. We had created something totally unique to our community. Explaining it to people walking by in the hall was a bit difficult, but we all knew what we were doing and why.

THE JOURNEY PROBLEM

I'm a geography nut. I could sit and look at maps and globes for hours. The kids know this, so the older ones weren't surprised when I thought up the Journey Problem. Being on an island in the middle of the Pacific Ocean provided a perfect opportunity for some great geography discussions.

This problem was a combination of math, geography, writing, and social studies. I also wanted it to offer some real-life problems and some surprises along the way.

This problem was originally called the Adventure Problem, and that is how it reads on the problem sheet. But over the course of the weeks we were working on it, the kids kept referring it to the Journey Problem, so now I do too (see Figure 13).

The Starting Point

I made books out of 11 x 17 inch white construction paper for the kids to use as journals. Inside, I glued a copy of the problem and a blank one-month calendar. The kids chose partners and the first thing the partners needed to do was to decide where they wanted to go. They wrote down what oceans, continents, and countries they would be traveling to. This opened up many great discussions.

"Jill, I'm going to go to Pennsylvania so I can learn more about the Civil War!" Dave was so excited, I hated to deflate him, but I did anyway.

"Dave, is Pennsylvania a country?"

"Oh, yeah. It's one of the states, isn't it? Well, since we're already in the United States, do I have to write it?"

"Are we in the United States? Is the island in the United States?"

"Oh, I guess not. Okay, I'll write the United States instead."

"That's okay, I know now what you mean and it will be fun for us to hear about Pennsylvania and what you learn there."

The kids were using maps, globes, and atlases to decide where they wanted to travel. I enjoy watching them figuring out geography. They have absolutely no idea how long it will take to get places. "We'll just kayak to China from Egypt," Carly wrote. For now, I let these comments slide by.

It took a few days for everyone to decide where they would be traveling. The next step was to schedule the travel time. I gave the children a choice of two or three weeks. They then decided what month their partnership wanted to leave and filled in their calendars. I asked them to write when they would be leaving and when they would be returning to the island on the calendar. The months varied, and that proved to be an important difference later on.

Journals

In these journals the kids recorded the adventures they were having on their trip. They made up stories about how they traveled to each new destination

ADVENTURE PROBLEM

You and your group are going on an adventure! All you have to do is follow the rules listed below! HAVE FUN AND BE CAREFUL ON YOUR ADVENTURE!

You need to start and end on our island. On your adventure, you need to pass through at least:

2 oceans, 2 continents, and 4 countries

Make and keep a journal.
Write down EXACTLY how you got to each place.
Write down EXACTLY the directions you went as you were travelling.
Write how long it took you to get to each place. (Remember how to figure out miles on a map?)
Write how long you spent at each place.
As you write, make up fun adventures you had along the way. Write about the types of animals you saw, the land forms you saw...

Here is your budget:

Your group gets $575 to spend on this trip.
Here are some things you need to keep in mind when you spend your money:
> Food for the day
> Renting boats, going on planes, (balloon rides!)...
> Special tours
> Emergency money
> Souvenirs
> ... and anything else you want.

You need to make a budget of what you spent daily. (Challenge yourself with the amounts!)
When you get back to the island, you need to have some money left. All the money needs to be divided up equally between the entire group.

MAKE SURE YOU KEEP GOOD RECORDS FOR YOUR MONEY!! YOU NEVER KNOW WHAT MIGHT HAPPEN!!

AND...

Upon returning home to the island, you need to show the rest of us the following items:
> 1. a "photo album" of your trip
> 2. at least 3 souvenirs that you bought
> 3. one adventure you had
> 4. a map of your journey
> 5. a copy of your budget

FIGURE 13   The Adventure (Journey) Problem.

and how they spent the money that had been allocated to them at the beginning of the trip (see Figure 14). They would make up stories about getting free food and places to sleep so they could save their money. They would write about people they met along the way and about souvenirs they had bought.

From Dave and Kiersten's journal: "That night we bought some scuba suits and went scuba diving. But an octopus grabbed Dave and almost killed him, but Kiersten shot him with a harpoon gun and Dave was OK. The hospital bill was $100. Now we have $11."

From Tessia and Laura's journal: "The boat was too slow, so we took a jet. It took 5 hours, and it was $75. The pilots were nice enough to let us have dinner free! So once again we did not have to spend for dinner. We ate dried seaweed and fried fish. The dried seaweed was disgusting! (But it was new!)" (See Figure 15.)

From JB and Carly's journal: "We bought 2 kayaks for $1 a piece. The reason it was so cheap was because we were the 10,000 customer. We kayaked in the Gulf of Mexico."

Besides thinking of ways to save money, the kids also encountered some obstacles. One morning, before school, I wrote a little story in everyone's journal—they had lost all their money. For example, in Zack and Kyle's journal I wrote: "While you were at your friend's house having dinner, the window was open. All your money blew away and the people in New York took it! You have NO money left. Now what will you do?"

Their response was, "We stopped by a nice old lady's house and we did some yard work and sold her some of Kyle's pictures and she gave us $66.99 and then we bought food. When we were walking we found a penny, so now we have $51."

In Carly and JB's journal I wrote: "As you were fishing, your wallet dropped into the water and sank! You have NO money left! What will you do now?" They wrote: "We sold our boat and got $5.41. We kayaked to China. It took us 1 day. We have $6 now. We go to China and Carly got a job to do gymnastics on the street. She got $59."

What thrilled me about the way they reacted to this problem was that they came up with such creative ways to earn their money back. We talked about the fact that losing your money is a real-life problem for many people who travel and about what you could do so it wouldn't happen to you.

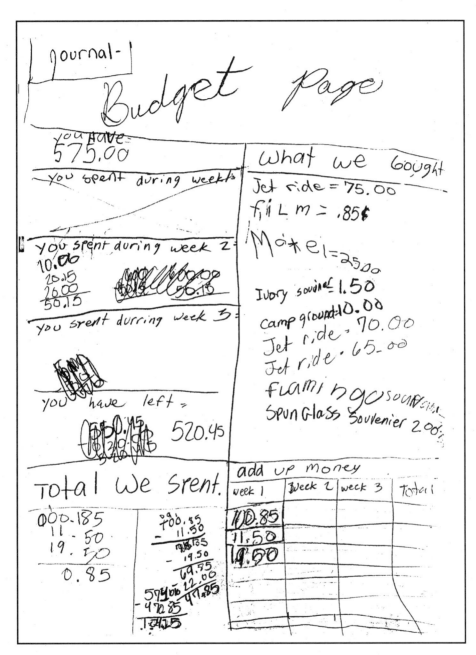

Journal-
Budget page

you have
575.00

you spent during weeks

you spent during week 2
10.00
20.15
26.00
56.15

you srent durring week 3

you have left =
520.45

What we bought

Jet ride = 75.00

fiLm = .85¢

Motel = 25.00

Ivory souvnier 1.50

camp ground 10.00

Jet ride = 70.00

Jet ride = 65.00

FLamingo souvenier

Spun Glass souvenier 2.00

Total We srent.

000.185
11. 50
19. 50
0.85

700.85
- 11.50
- 19.50
69.55
12.00
574.00 47.85
- 47.85
.TH25

add up money

week 1	week 2	week 3	Total
10.85			
11.50			
19.50			

FIGURE 14 Tessia and Laura's budget for their journey.

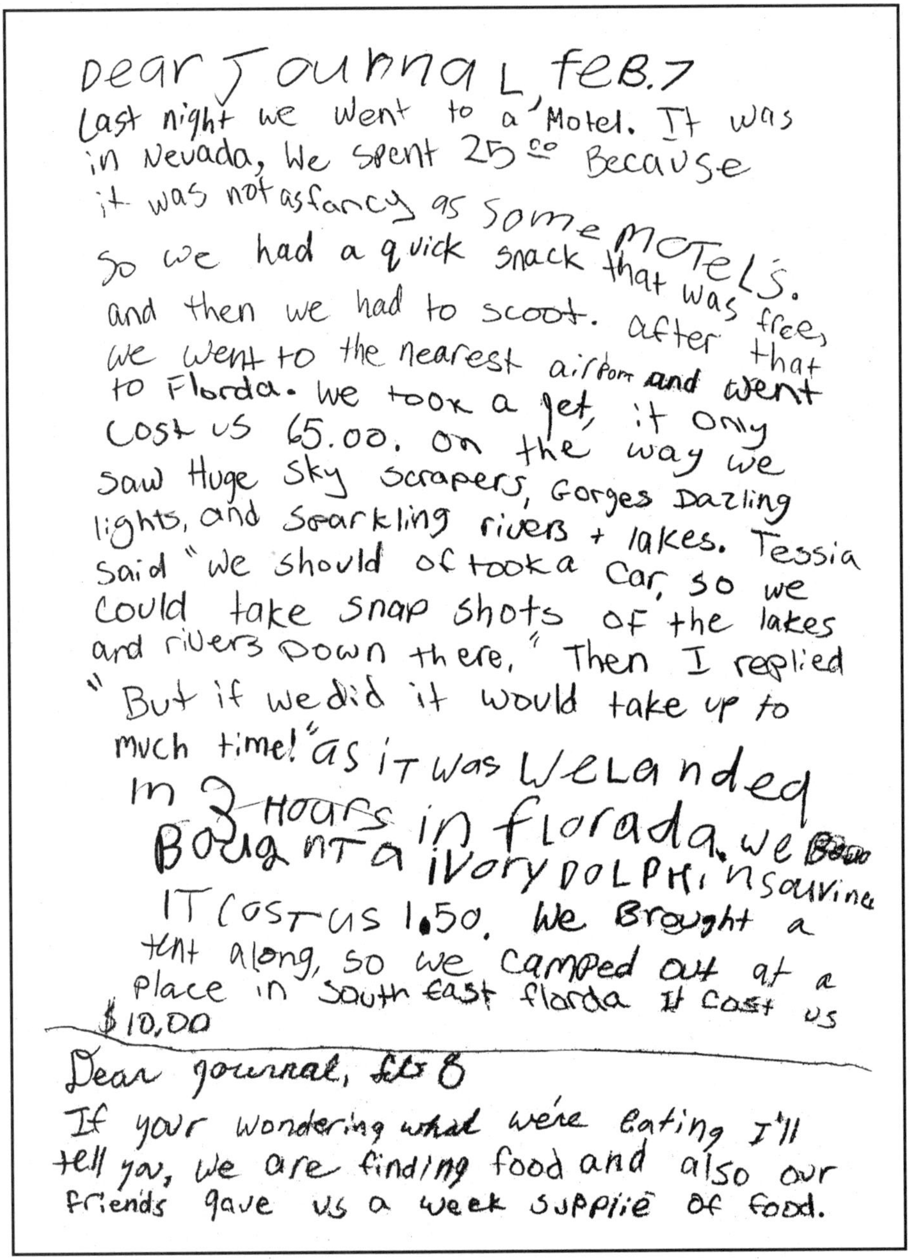

Dear Journal Feb.7
Last night we went to a Motel. It was in Nevada, We spent 25.00 because it was not as fancy as some MOTELS. So we had a quick snack that was free, and then we had to scoot. After that we went to the nearest airport and went to Florda. We took a jet, it only cost us 65.00. On the way we saw Huge Sky scrapers, Gorges Dazling lights, and Sparkling rivers + lakes. Tessia said "We should of took a car, so we could take snap shots of the lakes and rivers down there." Then I replied "But if we did it would take up to much time!" As it was WE LANDED In 3 Hours in florada. we Bought a ivory DOLPHIN Souvine It COST us 1.50. We Brought a tent along, so we camped out at a place in south east florda It cost us $10.00

Dear journal, Feb 8
If your wondering what we're eating I'll tell you, we are finding food and also our friends gave us a week supplie of food.

FIGURE 15   A journal entry.

Laura's watercolor image of our island classroom.

Our island meeting hut made out of carpet roll tubes and crepe paper (p.10).

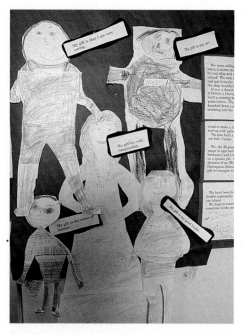

The hallway outside our classroom displays the kids' body pictures with their gifts (p.13).

The couches and chairs I've collected for the classroom make a comfortable environment and provide children with more choice for learning and sharing (p. 33).

The file cabinet provided a second opening into the hill and mountain structure we built (p. 34).

Our finished hill and mountain, complete with animals, flowers, a waterfall, and a trapdoor for storage (p. 35).

Planning our minpins parks outside in the school yard (p. 41).

Zack, a fifth grader, teaches a karate mini-class (p. 72).

4

A mini-class on how to make nests (p. 72).

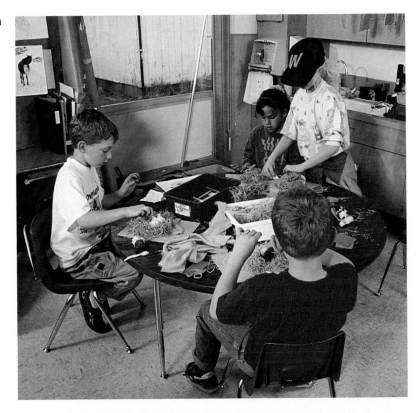

The kids made dioramas for the festivals they researched. This one is for the Carnival festival (p. 78).

Carnival

A page from Zack and Kyle's journal shows some of the clothes they bought and talks about the places they went on their trip (p. 85).

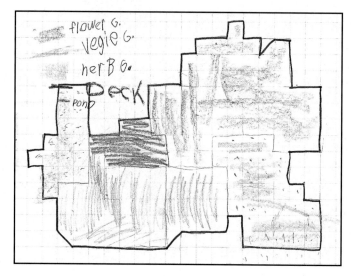

Dave and Rachel made a color key to help them plot their garden on the small graph paper (p. 93).

The garden plans were transferred from small graph paper to large graph paper. The plans were then transferred to colored construction paper showing each garden, and the pieces fit together like a puzzle. The black paper shows the paths connecting the gardens (p. 94).

Dave painted a watercolor of someone walking down the garden path (p. 100).

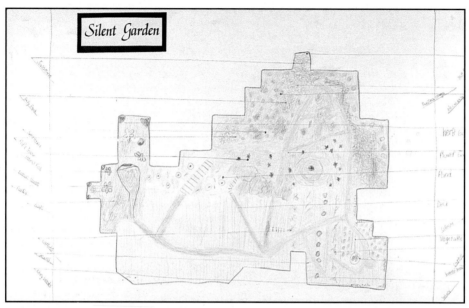

We labeled the final board for the Silent Garden with the names of the individual gardens and plants (p. 101).

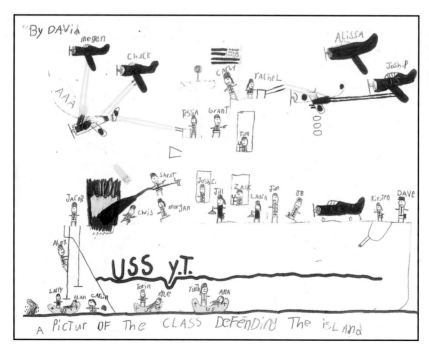

David's picture of the class defending "Ostrow's Outrageous Island."

"Well, people shouldn't leave their money on the table by an open window like Zack and Kyle did."

"Some people don't carry cash on trips with them."

Another thing I asked the kids to do in their journals was to write a letter to someone. The letters, which were glued into their journals in little envelopes, were quite funny.

When they returned to the island, I asked them to make a map showing where they had traveled. Some kids traced real maps, and some kids drew freehand. Then they glued them into their journals (see Figure 16).

Presentations

After everyone had "returned home," we began to think about how we would share the journals. We all decided to include these items in the presentations:

- the countries you went through
- the oceans you passed over
- your favorite adventure
- the most expensive thing you bought
- how much money you had left
- how much each of you got back at the end
- your souvenir
- your photo album

We talked about possible ways to present their journeys. "What are some ideas?" I asked the whole group.

"We could do a play," said someone.

"Or a puppet show," said another.

"Or, we could do a speech."

"Just so it's creative!" chimed in Tessia.

"Well, I don't think it *needs* to be creative. I mean, if you want to stand up there and read from the list of requirements, you can. But what will happen to the audience?"

"They'll probably get bored," Tessia shared.

"Yeah, maybe, but it's still a choice you have if you can't think of another way to share your stuff." I knew of one partnership for sure that would have a difficult time figuring out a way to share, and I wanted them to be sure they knew that reading from their requirement sheet was an option.

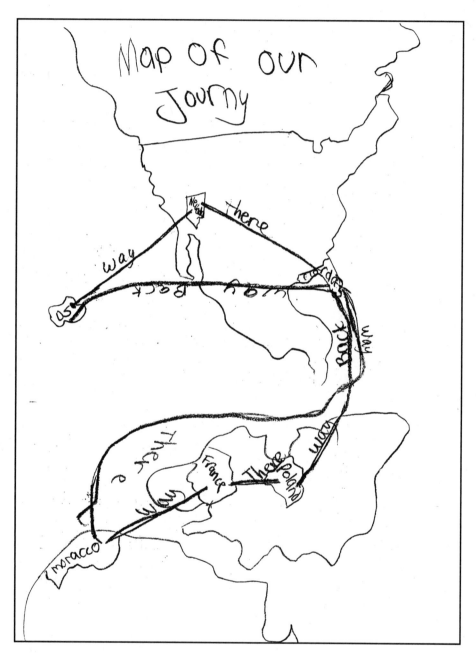

FIGURE 16 The map of Tessia and Laura's journey.

Three partnerships presented their project in a talk show format. Laura and Tessia presented this way. Laura was the talk show host.

"Now, Tessia, can you tell us what countries you traveled to on your journey?"

"Why yes, I can. We went to the U.S., France, Poland, and Morocco." The talk show continued like this for their entire presentation. It was a great way to present information. I don't remember it ever being done that way before, but it sure was popular.

Rachel and Megan presented their journey in a more dramatic form. They made large signs with the names of the countries and each time they talked about a new country, they held up that sign.

Zack and Kyle did something completely different and unusual. They presented most of their journey by straight forward telling, but they also put on a skit about their favorite adventure: when they lost all their money. For their props, they made a scene of a New York street from a bird's-eye view. They drew shops along it and made the road itself black with white street lines down the center. It was wonderful. Their skit showed the money falling onto the street below.

During the presentations, it was easy for me to check to see which kids had a clear understanding of the difference between countries and continents. I didn't *teach* the difference; the kids figured it out by using maps and globes and constantly sharing and discussing. I was taught geography by memorizing places on a map or globe. It seems so much more appropriate and helpful to have kids actually doing something that is *real*, or close to real!

THE GARDEN PROBLEM

The kids were interested in the house I had recently bought, and were constantly asking me about my progress with the garden that spring. In response to their interest, I wrote the Garden Problem. We connected it to our island study by pretending we each had a plot of land we wanted use for a garden.

The Garden Problem was similar to the pond and forest problems we had done the year before. These are long, time-consuming, extremely challenging problems that I don't present until April. The kids work on similar smaller problems throughout the year, but I wait until they have had all the experience they can before they undertake something this involved (see Figure 17).

GARDEN PROBLEM

You will be designing a garden spot. Here are your requirements:
- You get 175 square feet of land for your garden.
- Your space CANNOT be a perfect square.
- You will need the following items in your garden:

a vegetable garden   a flower garden

an herb garden   a deck

- You will need a place where tall trees will provide shade.
- Your flower spot does not need to only be in one spot.

Here is how much space each area needs to be:

vegetable garden--1/5 of total space   flower garden--3/10 of total space

herb garden--1/10 of total space   play area and deck--3/10 of total space

You can use any extra space any way you wish.

You will need a path connecting all gardens.

> DESIGN YOUR GARDEN USING THE ABOVE SPECIFICATIONS.

THEN...

Before you pick your items to plant, you will need the following:

Flowers: 1/2 need to be perennials

1/2 need to be annuals

Vegetables: 2/5 need to be greens

2/5 need to be underground veggies

1/5 need to be vine or above ground

Herbs: You need 4 different types of herbs.

Play area and deck: Just grass for play area. There must be some shade from 3 different types of fruit trees.

Decide on your plants, THEN...

Here's your budget. You get to spend $150 on your plants.

Price List

perennials, pack of 5--$5.00   annuals, pack of 5--$5.00

herb starters, each--$1.50   trees, each--$15.00

Get as close to $150 as you can!

Write up your budget sheet neatly and write how you added everything up.

THEN...

Name your garden.

Write a poem about your garden.

Paint a watercolor of your garden.

THEN...

PRESENT YOUR GARDEN!

FIGURE 17 The Garden Problem.

This problem occupied the kids for more than three weeks. The kids worked as partners, choosing someone of a different age or gender to work with. We did some parts of the problem together as a large group, the kids did other parts at their own pace, and we also approached it through mini-lessons. Throughout the entire time, the one thing we did constantly—as we always do—is share our ideas.

The Garden Problem includes math, writing, reading, botany, and art. The math component, for example, uses square footage, measurement, multiplication, fractions, equivalent fractions, design, money, and estimation. When a problem consists of so many concepts, mini-lessons are imperative. But I also wanted the kids to figure out how to solve certain parts of it on their own. Such was the case for the first step—figuring out the square footage.

The Small Graph Paper Draft

Each garden plot had to be 175 square feet. The kids used quarter-inch graph paper to figure this out and came up with various solutions.

Dave and Rachel: "We went 10 x 10 is 100, so then we went 10 x 7 is 70. We had 170 and just added 5 more."

Jacob and Chris: "Well, we made a line of 10 squares and then counted ten of them and that was 100, 'cause 10 tens is 100. Then we needed 75 more, so . . . so we counted 75 squares. And we got 175."

JB and Kyle: "I knew that 17 x 10 is 170, so I just added 5 more." JB, a third grader, is able to solve numerical problems quickly. It was easy for him to see that 17 x 10 was 170. But Kyle, his partner, is a first grader. He didn't understand what JB was doing and couldn't keep up with him. This is another reason why whole group share times are so important. Luckily, Kyle was able to listen to Jacob and Chris and understand exactly how they got their 175 square feet. Another partnership simply counted out 175 squares. There is something for everyone during these share times.

From the Pond Problem the year before some of the kids remembered how to change the shape of the plan but still keep it 175 square feet. "If you take 10 squares from the inside, just add 10 squares to the outside," JB explained to Kyle. All the garden plans looked different. Some were "squarelike," while others took very complex shapes.

After all the kids had outlined their garden on small graph paper, they needed to figure out how much space each of the individual areas for vegetables, flowers, and herbs would need. This caused quite a dilemma, since I had specified fractions that were not equivalent. We had a whole group mini-lesson on how to solve this problem.

"Well, they are all in tenths except the vegetable garden," someone commented. "So, maybe that one should just be half?"

"Half of what? And why half?" I questioned. Many blank faces stared back at me. I asked everyone go get a piece of paper and two crayons, and meet me back at the platform. "Okay," I began. (This was helpful to me because I was always terrible at converting fractions as a child.) "Fold your paper in half. Now fold it in half again. What fraction did we fold the paper into?"

"Fourths," someone said.

"Good, now color in two-fourths. How many squares is that, Kyle?" I like to give some of the younger kids time to answer questions the older kids can answer quickly. We talk a lot about giving "thinking-time" to everyone.

"Two."

"Now, write two-fourths on the paper somewhere. With your other crayon, draw a line down one of your folds. How many pieces are on either side of the fold, Kiersten?"

"Two."

"And how many of those pieces did you color in?"

"One."

"Hey, that's one-half!" Dave shouted.

"Yeah, what does this tell you about two-fourths?"

"It's the same as one-half," Laura said. We did more problems like this together as a group, and then I sent them off to see if they could figure out how many tenths one-fifth would be. When we met again to share solutions, some kids had done paper folding, others had used unifix cubes, and still others had figured it out in their heads.

The next step was determining the actual amount of space they needed for each garden, given the requirements I had set down. Everyone changed the one-fifth to two-tenths for the vegetable garden. Then they worked with their partners to figure out the amounts. This was one part of the problem for which I purposely did not offer a mini-lesson. I knew it was difficult, but I wanted to see how they went about solving it. Many kids counted out 175 cubes and divided them into ten groups. The additional 5 became their extra space. Zack did an elaborate picture with graph paper and counted-out squares, but JB came up with the amounts first.

"Jill, we've got it. We have the numbers." I went over to see and noticed a crowd around us. I hadn't intended that this to be a large group share, but most of the kids were tired of counting cubes and just wanted the numbers. They recorded JB's numbers on their problem sheet.

What struck me was JB's generosity in sharing his answers after he had worked so hard on them, but also how the kids felt about using them. No one said, "That's cheating!" The kids were all working hard, so why not get the figures from JB? For me, it demonstrated community cooperation and respect.

Using JB's figures, the kids made rough draft plans of their gardens. Dave and Rachel even made a color key, which inspired the rest of the partnerships to follow suit (see insert page 6).

The Large Graph Paper Draft

After they had made their small drafts, they needed to transfer their plans onto larger one-inch graph paper. (I have one-inch graph paper that comes in chart paper size.) This was more difficult than it seemed. The children had to be very careful counting the squares and know which parts they had already counted. As I walked around observing, I discovered many different approaches to organization.

Josh and Chuck took turns counting a side and filling it in on the large graph paper. Tessia and Megan marked their draft so they wouldn't count the same side twice by mistake. David counted out the number of squares, and Rachel drew them in on the large paper.

After the one-inch graph paper gardens were complete and darkly outlined, the kids shared them with the whole class. I let them have a question and comment time to talk about any part of the problem so far.

This graph paper work took three days. The next part, which I had assumed would be fairly easy, turned out to be one of the most difficult parts of the entire problem.

To make sharing our designs easier, I wanted all the smaller gardens on their one-inch graph paper to be the same color. For instance, if we were talking about the herb garden, I thought it might be easier if all the herb gardens were orange. That way, when the children held up their draft, we would all recognize where the herb garden was. Simply coloring in each garden would have been easy, but of course I suggested something extremely challenging. As a group we chose construction paper in five colors: the herb garden would be orange, the flower garden purple, the vegetable garden green, the deck yellow, and the extra space blue. The children had to measure each garden and make it exactly the same size on the construction paper. When they finished, all five pieces of construction paper should fit together onto their graph paper draft like a puzzle.

Ruth Hubbard was there the day the class worked on this, and we were both amazed at how difficult it was—and not just for the kids but for us too. They knew that the graph paper was marked off in one-inch squares, so they used rulers to measure the sides of their gardens. The hard part was measuring some of the more complex designs. I helped many of the teams because they needed help, but some had no trouble at all, which also amazed me (see insert page 7).

The Flowers

Now we were ready to look at plantings for the gardens. "Does anyone know what the difference between an annual and a perennial is?" No response. "Oh, well, I guess we can't finish the problem. One-half of the flowers need to be annuals and one-half perennials, and if you don't know, we can't continue. Too bad." Luckily, the kids are familiar with my warped sense of humor and said right away, "Yeah, right Jill."

"Well, how are you going to find out?"

"Ask somebody or look in a book," said a chorus of voices. Rachel said she could find out because her mom was a landscape architect. I told the kids I'd give them a day to find out and we'd choose flowers the next day.

The following day, Rachel came in knowing the difference between annuals and perennials, and so did a handful of other children. They explained the difference to the rest of the class, and we started the next step of the problem.

Because I had been working on my own garden, I had acquired a number of books about gardening. I brought some of these in to class so the kids could look at different kinds of flowers before they made their choices. They did observational drawings of some and dissected flowers to observe the different parts. What was important to me at this point was having the kids group the flowers they liked into one of two categories: annuals and perennials.

We decided that I would hold up one of the books and show pictures of various flowers. When someone saw a flower they liked, they wrote its name down on a piece of paper. First one-half of the class chose their flowers, then the other. This worked out nicely because those not choosing could work on their construction paper cutouts.

We went through all the perennials and then began on the annuals. This turned out to be very time consuming. There were hundreds of flowers. If I were to do this again, I would leave the flower collection up to the kids. I did it this way because we didn't have many good flower books in our school library, and I had borrowed books from a close friend, which I didn't want the kids handling. In the long run, it worked out, and the kids figured out ways to make it easier. Some realized, for example, that they needed to record the color of the flower so they wouldn't forget what it looked like. Laura suggested that we change the required proportion of the annuals.

"If we have one-half annuals, then every spring we'd have to plant one-half of the garden. Why not have three-fourths perennials and one-fourth annuals?" She shared her idea with the rest of the class and everyone agreed.

When we were finished choosing flowers, the kids had two long lists. They worked with their partners to highlight the flowers they wanted in their garden and cross out those they didn't want.

When it came time for figuring out the fractions, we met to discuss how to do it.

"How will you know how many of each flower you need?" I asked them. "What is the first thing you need to know in order to make a fraction?"

"What the whole group is," answered Grant.

"Okay, so let's say I have sixteen cubes. How can I find out what three-fourths is?" I looked toward Morgan, a second grader. "Morgan, what does the bottom number mean in a fraction? Do you remember?"

"Um, how many groups?"

"Good! So, how many groups should I make with my sixteen cubes?"

"Four."

"Okay. Now what, Caitlin?" I asked a first-grade girl.

"I can't remember."

"Why did I split the group into four smaller groups?"

"'Cause it was the bottom number. Oh, yeah, the top number you pick up. Pick up three groups." And I grabbed three groups of cubes.

"Megan, will you count these for me?"

"There are twelve."

"So, what's three-fourths of sixteen?"

"Twelve."

"JB, what would one-fourth of sixteen be?"

"Four."

"So, how would you figure out the amounts of annuals and perennials you need?"

Laura offered a suggestion: "First, you need a whole group. So, count up all your flowers. Then, take three-fourths of that number for perennials and one-fourth of that number to get your annuals."

"Sounds good to me. Go." And off they went to solve this problem. What they found was that they needed to cut more flowers from their original lists. They also played around with the numbers: if they had a total number of seventeen, they would take away a flower instead of dealing with an uneven number.

After their work on the flowers, the kids could work pretty independently on choosing the vegetables. As partners continued working on the flower and vegetable fractions, I decided to introduce herbs to the kids to give them a break from their fraction work. I had bought eight different types of herbs. I let the kids smell and touch them, draw the entire plant, draw a single leaf, and predict what each herb was. We talked about growth, roots, and the amount of sun the herbs required. This science observation took most of a morning. The following day, the kids chose their herbs from those they had observed and others they hadn't. The only requirement was to end up with four different types of herbs.

The Final Board

Now it was time to transfer the large graph paper draft onto a final board. I had initially wanted to mount each garden plan on a piece of foam board, but that turned out to be too expensive. I ended up with art board, which is thicker than poster board but cheaper than foam board. I explained to the kids that they would only get one piece per set of partners, so they had to work carefully. We talked about "mess-ups" and how they could avoid them, about how to use the art erasers, and about ways to transfer the large draft onto the board. Before the children began to transfer their drafts, I asked them to draw a line down the sides of the board three inches in from the edge to make a space where the labels would go. When they had completed that, we met together on the platform to discuss transferring the draft.

"What are some ways you could do it?" I asked the group.

"You could trace it. But then we'd have to cut it out."

"That's okay, you can cut it out." The draft was still on the large graph paper.

"We could measure it," someone else suggested.

"You could. It might be hard to do that, but it certainly is an option."

"We could eyeball it like we do sometimes for observational drawing," said another.

"Wow, eyeballing would be so difficult for me, but I bet it would be easier for some of you!"

"Yeah, like Kyle!" This is where Kyle took over in his partnership with JB. He looked at their draft and drew the exact same shape onto the board. It was quite amazing to watch. Grant and Caitlin took days to transfer their draft onto the board because they were measuring with a ruler. Most of the partnerships cut out and traced their drafts onto the board. The partners completed this step at different times over several days. After they had transferred the drafts, they outlined the garden with a black colored pencil.

The Bank

During the time they were transferring their drafts onto the board, I had set aside a day for them to do their "buying." The problem stated that they had $150 to spend on plants and included a price list for the flowers, herbs, and trees. (They asked me how much the vegetables were. I had forgotten to add those, so I told them they were free. They liked that!)

I acted as the bank. I gave each partnership $150 in play paper money. I gave them each large bills—only fifties, twenties, and tens. Their job was to figure out how much they were going to spend on each item and send one partner to the bank if they needed change. I made a rule that only the younger partner could come to the bank. That way, I was able to question them about their knowledge of money.

What a morning! Dave and Rachel lost $10 along the way and were trying desperately to figure out what had gone wrong. I was very busy at the bank. Many of the kids ended up with change because sometimes I would give out coins instead of bills. I would also give out the wrong amount of change, cautioning them to check their money. I was caught every time.

When they had counted out all their money, they made up budget sheets showing what they had spent. Most of the kids organized their budget according to how they spent their money: flowers first, then the herbs, and so on. I never checked to see if their budget sheets were "correct"; correctness wasn't my objective. Learning to handle large amounts of money and make change and work in partnership was much more important to me.

When the budget sheets were complete, the children stapled the money they had spent onto the sheet. Everyone's budget sheets looked different. I didn't give out blank paper or tell them how to set it up; they just invented a way that was be appropriate for their own use. After the money day, the kids went back to working on their gardens (see Figure 18).

Drawing

We met as a whole group one day to talk about drawing in the details of the garden.

"What do you think we should use?" I asked.

"Really good pencils and those yellow erasers." I put sharp new pencils and art erasers out in a special tub specifically for use on the gardens.

One thing they were required to draw in was a path connecting all the individual gardens. I asked them to go back to their big draft and make the path in black. Some kids drew it with black crayon, and others used black strips of construction paper. The path would eventually be drawn onto the final board.

When the first set of partners had completed the pencil drawings of the entire garden, we met again as a group to talk about the colored pencils. I had borrowed top quality colored pencils from another teacher, and I explained to the children how to use them. I was firm as I was explaining this, making sure they understood that they needed to take their time and be careful, and they respected my concern. I showed them how to go over a spot with the pencil many times to get the desired tone, instead of pressing hard with the pencil. Using colored pencils in that way was new to them. For the next week and a half, the kids worked on drawing and coloring in their gardens.

They were gorgeous. I had never seen such careful work before. The detail and the way they were using the colored pencils was incredible. Some of the kids used shades of brown and gray to make their paths look like stone walkways. The coloring took a long time. The amount of time we spent on them during the day varied. Sometimes we would work as a whole class for an hour; on other days kids would work on them independently.

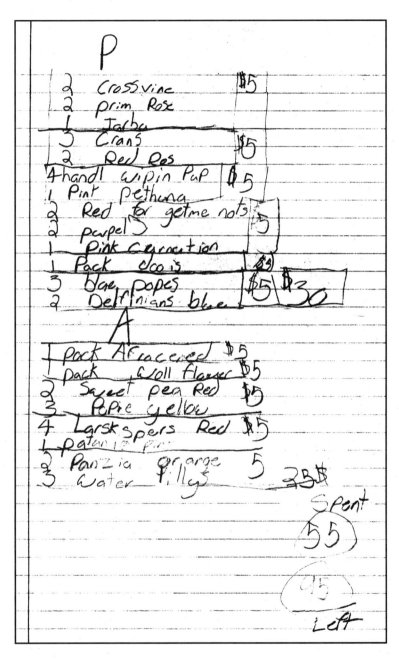

P

2	Crossvine	$5
2	prim Rose	
1	Jarbu	
3	Crans	$5
2	Red Ros	
4 handl	wipin PuP	$5
1	Pint Pethuna	
2	Red for getme nots	$5
2	purpel	
1	Pink carnation	
1	Pack deois	
3	blue popes	$5 $30
2	Delrinians blue	

A

1	Pack Afraceaed	$5
1	pack Woll Flower	$5
2	Sweet pea Red	$5
3	Popie yellow	
4	Larskspers Red	$5
1	Patunia Pin	
2	Panzia orange	5
3	Water Lillys	35$

Spent
55

45

Left

FIGURE 18   Rachel's breakdown of the $150 flower budget.

Watercolors and Poems

We had discussed *perspective* and *point of view* constantly throughout the year. When the children went to paint a watercolor of their garden, I invited them to do it from any perspective they choose. Later, when they shared their paintings with the whole class, we should be able to clearly see where the "artist's eye" was.

For this kind of artwork I use real watercolors, the kind that come in tubes. I buy a box of eighteen colors, and these usually last almost the entire year. The kids learn how to use just a drop of paint and mix it with lots of water.

The paintings were as varied as the kids. Zack painted from the perspective of lying down on the grass; in the center of his painting a huge leg was walking by. Morgan painted from a bird's-eye view. Dave painted a side view: the artist's eye was looking at someone walking down the path (see insert page 7).

As the kids were painting, they were also working on poems to go with their gardens. We decided to write descriptive poems.

> Flowers blooming with a woosh
>> Bright yellow
> Wind blowing
>> Bent flower
> Trees shivering
>>> shhhh
> Green leaves falling
> Lily pad bobbing
> People walking on the path
>> Looking at the scenery
> Ooohing, aaahing with excitement
>> DAVID

> Flowers blooming
>> Pop pop
> Red
>> Yellow
>>> Blue
>>> Pink
> Flower-scented meadows

Fountain shimmering
    Shining
        Splashing
Herb-scented designs
    Basil
        Tea leaf
            Sage
Pick pick veggies
Smells of tomatoes
    Onions . . . ee-yew
Birds shivering in the swaying tree
Me running
    Drip
        Drom
            Drim
                Drop
RACHEL

Labeling

The last bit of work to be done on the board was the labeling. We agreed that it would be impractical to label every flower and vegetable, so I let them choose three or four. They would, however, need to label all the individual gardens and the deck. Earlier, I had asked them to leave a three-inch space down each side. This was the space in which the labels went. They neatly wrote the names of the gardens and plants in this space (see insert page 8).

Reflections

After all the gardens were completed, I asked each child to write a reflection. One question I asked them to think about was what the most difficult part of the problem was for them and how they went about solving it. They were quite honest in these responses. I suppose I was thinking that most of the kids would mention the construction paper cutouts, but this was not the case for a majority of the class. I also asked them to write what math they needed to know in order to do the Garden Problem.

Carly wrote: "I think the hardest part of the Garden Problem was buying the plants. We had to figure out lots of stuff. So we took turns figuring it out. The math we used to solve it was mostly + and −. We needed to know lots of stuff like fractions and money."

Dave wrote: "1. The hardest part was when we lost our money. 2. The way we solved it was a loan from the bank. 3. We used math adding and fractions."

Jacob wrote: "The hardest part was making the path. I looked at the plan. Counting money, splitting up groups."

Grant had a very honest reflection: "The hard part for me was when Caitlin (his partner) would not work and I told her to use her brain and to think about what she was doing. So she is trying a little bit harder so that makes me happy. I needed to know fractions and times to figure out how to get the right space for different gardens." The kids are constantly writing about how they solved problems, but they had rarely reflected on their work like this. Their responses showed me how important reflection is, and I am determined to do more of it in the future.

Presentations

Our favorite time was the presentations. We decided to have two sets of partners share a day—one in the morning and one in the afternoon, so we wouldn't get "bored." I made a calendar and the kids signed up for a time they wanted.

I wanted the kids to have the experience of assessing each other's work, so before we began we made a list of all of the important things we would be looking for. I typed the list up and made copies it for the kids to use. I asked the partners to use the form to do a self-evaluation first. That way, they would be familiar with it when they listened to the other children's presentations.

First up were Alan and Morgan. The rest of us sat on the platform with our evaluation sheets clipped to our clipboards (the kids and I all have a clipboard) eagerly awaiting their presentation. What I heard during this presentation, however, was the audience!

"Wait, what did he say? I missed that."

"Slow down, I can't write that fast."

"Is there a path, yep, okay go on." The kids were so busy filling out their forms, they weren't hearing what Alan and Morgan were saying. The youngest kids were totally frustrated. What a flop! And what an important lesson we learned.

When Alan and Morgan were finished, we all talked about the evaluation forms. "All I was looking at was what was on the form. I didn't even listen to what they were talking about. It was dumb," Grant said. He was right. We talked about what we thought would have happened if I had given out this form before we began our work on the problem.

"Oh, we probably would have done only what was on the sheet and they probably wouldn't have turned out as good," Tessia commented. I agreed. This is why I am uncomfortable with rubrics. They seem to put a cap on what is possible. Kids focus on how many points they can get, or whether they did everything right, instead of focusing on the actual project. I also worry that using some rubrics will result in similar-looking projects.

After our discussion of the evaluation forms, we talked about other ways we could evaluate the project. Dave suggested that we write something about the presentation. That led into a discussion of the narrative reports I write on the kids instead of the standard report card. They suddenly realized why those are so important. "They tell us and our parents so much more than just a number," Tessia explained. "Bingo," I said.

The kids then came up with three types of evaluation they wanted to write for the Garden Problem after the partners had done their presentations. They wanted to:

1. Write a narrative on their own.
2. Write a narrative in a small group.
3. Write a narrative as a whole group.

We decided to write two individual narratives, two narratives in a small group, and two large group narratives, and the kids could pick the one they wanted to write about.

Dave and Rachel presented their garden, and the kids went off to write their responses. Alissa wrote: "It was very neat. The lines were straight. Dave's watercolor was neat. His poem was descriptive."

Torin wrote: "Dave's poem was read with expression and in a loud voice. The path was neat. You could see all the gardens."

JB wrote: "The way they got their 175 square feet was weird. Because first they did a 10 x 7 square to get 70 then they added 100 then they added 5. Dave's watercolor was great because you could see the perspective and it was beautiful. Dave's poem was very descriptive and he read with expression. The way they organized their money and what they bought was good."

After Jacob and Chris presented, Alissa, Alan, and JB wrote: "Fractions were a bit off but the way they solved it was interesting. The final was colorful.

Both the watercolors had the same perspective. They had no budget sheet or no key on the little plan. Jacob's explanation of 175 was very good. Chris read loud. Both need more expression."

Grant, Kiersten, and Morgan wrote: "I like how they made the bridge and I like their watercolors and I like Chris's shadow. I like the way Chris made a shadow of a person. I think that this is their best art they have ever done because it is so neat."

Zack and Torin's whole group evaluation was more like a discussion. I took notes as the kids shared their thoughts. "Zack's poem was descriptive. We could see where the artist's eye was in both watercolors. Torin read really well. The final board was neat. The houses were great. The poems were descriptive. The fractions were accurate, but the gardens weren't. The lines were straight. The draft was neat. The board was colorful."

Our assessment of these projects was not limited to the presentations. The kids and I were constantly assessing throughout their work on the garden. We were simply analyzing different aspects of the problem. Grant assessed his work with a difficult partner and wrote about it in his evaluation. I was constantly observing the amount of independence the kids were achieving. As a class we talked about how to assess. Assessment is not something I do just at the end of a project. It's an ongoing aspect of teaching and learning.

Plotting to Scale

We wanted to take the Garden Problem a bit further and see just how big 175 square feet really was. I didn't think we would have room in our school's outdoor field to plot all twelve of the gardens, so we needed to decide on one. We voted for one that would be easy to plot but would also offer a challenge. The Silent Garden, Dave and Rachel's design, won.

I took the small draft of the Silent Garden and redrew it on one-fourth-inch graph paper. Then I took a pen and went around the outline of the plan marking off sections each set of partners would be responsible for plotting. I told the kids to bring a book or their Quiet Writing books outside so they could work on them while I was helping to plot the garden.

The kids had been collecting sticks to use as stakes to attach the string to. We started out fine, but halfway through the plotting, I messed up by going out when I should have gone in, and we had to pull off half the string and start again. (That was very frustrating!) In the end, the string-to-scale garden looked exactly like Dave and Rachel's garden. What struck me and the children most was how small 175 square feet is. I am terrible at estimating square footage, so I was expecting it to be huge. How wrong I was! We talked about all the flowers and vegetables we had expected to fit into that little space. "No way!" The kids made labels out of index cards to show where each garden was and attached those to a stake inside the string. From that, we were able to estimate other amounts of square footage. We could imagine what eight hundred or three thousand square feet would look like. JB went home and looked up how many square feet a football field would be.

OUTCOMES

This problem grew beyond the limit of the original Garden Problem. Often with problems such as this, things need to be added or taken away, depending on the situation. I hadn't intended to do the evaluations, or have a "bank day," or investigate herbs, or plot the garden to scale outside until we were well into it. I have learned to be flexible during these long, involved projects.

Projects like this reinforce the sense of choice, challenge, and independence the children learn and practice during workshop times, but they are different from a workshop in that they combine a number of concepts that correspond to what we are studying in class.

Choice

The children take ownership of these projects and become very engaged in them because they are meaningful to them and to our classroom community. During the Garden Problem presentation, the kids knew that evaluating each other's projects with check-off sheets was totally inappropriate. They were able to think of other options that would make it easier and more helpful for the entire group. Everyone also had a strong sense of ownership during the Holiday Research because we knew that at the end, we would be creating our own holiday. The children were motivated to work not only because they were interested in other cultures, but because they knew what the outcome would be.

Taking ownership of one's work falls along the same axis as being able to make choices. If children aren't able to choose for themselves, their ownership of their work somehow means less. During the Holiday Research presentations, the children could decide how to present their research to the class. They were very serious about these presentations, and I doubt that they would have been nearly as interesting had I made the requirements similar. The same held true for the presentations of the Journey Problem, which ranged from puppet shows to TV interviews.

Being able to decide how to solve the specific problems that arose during the projects was also important. There wasn't much room for individual choice in the Garden presentations because I had decided to have the kids assess each other. I thought it might be easier if the presentations were similar. Yet, the problem presented them with a number of decisions. Figuring out the 175 square feet inspired many approaches. Dave and Rachel figured 10 x 10 and then 10 x 7 and added 5 more. Jacob and Chris drew a 10 x 10 square and counted by ones to 75. JB knew that 17 x 10 was 170 and just added 5 more. This flexibility is not only important for the kids, it is important for me as well. This way I know exactly where each of the kids is in terms of his or her knowledge of a particular mathematical concept. Had I not allowed choice, I would not have known that JB could figure out 17 x 10 or that Chris and Jacob needed to count to 75.

The kids were also able to choose what flowers they wanted in their gardens. How unfair if I had made that choice for them. Yet some of their choices, such as the transfer of the draft of the garden onto the large board, were limited. The kids came up with the three options: measuring, tracing, or eyeballing the draft onto the board. Having that discussion showed me the options the kids had in mind. Had I followed my own decision, I probably would have told them to cut out the draft and trace it onto the board, because that seemed the easiest to me. But what I am learning from these children is that what is challenging to me isn't always challenging to them.

Challenges

The problems presented many challenges the children were asked to think about. Coming up with their presentation for their Holiday Research was a big job to some: many of the groups needed to bring in materials, food, and objects from home. This proved to be a challenging organizational task for some groups—who would bring in what and how. I had assumed the challenge I had added to their Journey journals—losing all their money—would be a major one for everyone. The interesting thing to watch, as they thought about it with their partners, was how resourceful they were. JB and Carly decided that Carly would perform gymnastics in the street and collect money from people walking by. Some of the kids decided to ask Jim Whitney, the photographer who takes pictures in the room, to send them money. Even when faced with this real-life dilemma, the kids came up with ways to solve it.

Some challenges do prove too much for some, and in that case, I offer a choice. During the final labeling of the gardens, putting a label on every plant and flower proved challenging—and inappropriate. Some partners challenged themselves to label as many as they could; others labeled two of everything. Another challenge was drawing the angled lines for the labels. This too became an individual decision. Some children chose to label using the angled lines, others to draw straight lines and write their labels on those.

Independence

All these problems call for independent work. Organizing their Holiday Research took independence in that I did not specify any particular method for organizing. Anna and Steve, for example, read notes from Anna's father, while JB, Josh, and Sharat read from books and took notes on their own. Coming up with a way out of their money crisis during the Journey Problem took a lot of initiative. They had to use their own experience and knowledge to find a way out. They couldn't come to me and say, "I don't know what to do" because they knew I wouldn't be able or willing to offer them any help.

The children know that most projects I give them will involve choice, challenge, and independence, which is why I rarely hear comments such as "I can't do this" or "He's cheating" or "Do I have to do it that way?" What I do hear is, "We can try it a different way if that doesn't work" or "I've got a way to solve it; does anyone want to see?"

In the end, because of their experience with these complex problems and projects, the children are able to create new ones for themselves. They learn to challenge themselves in their writing by adding more description or by writing stronger leads. They challenge themselves mathematically by solving a problem in more than one way. Recently, Caitlin came to show me five different ways she found to solve one simple problem. The kids also learn to write their own problems. After the Garden Problem, I asked some of the kids to make up

baseball
problem

You have to design a baseball stadium.
You have 800,000 square feet for the stadium and parking lot.
You need at least three 8x16 concession stands, how many square feet is an 8x16 square?
You need at least one 30x8 souvenir stand. How many square feet is a 30x8 square?
There shood be about 11,000 parking spots.
There needs to be about 35,000 seats.
You need to include lights, they need to be one foot tall.
You need to make 9 men to go on the field. They need to be 1/10 the size of the lights.
You need at least three 8x4 ticket booths.
You need a 10x6 scoreboard, it needs to be 11 inches tall.
Take a piece of graph paper and draw the stadium, but when you draw the stadium, each square is 10,000 square feet.

And

Then draw a picture of the stadium. When you are done with your draft do a final, and water color it.
Name your stadium.
Write a story about how your stadium got its name.

Oh, I almost forgot, the reason why I said the scoreboard needs to be 11 inches tall is because the stadium that you drew on the graph paper is going to be 3D.

HAVE FUN!!!

FIGURE 19   JB's Baseball Problem.

and do a project for a homework assignment. Their problems were complex and challenging, and created from their own interests (see Figure 19).

When I talk about these projects, especially the Garden Problem, at workshops and conferences, one of the first questions I am asked is, "Can we get a copy of that?" It always surprises me that anyone would want a copy. If I did give out copies and teachers tried to do the project with their kids, it would probably fail. These problems grew out of what our class was studying. It would be meaningless for someone to try to take on the Garden Problem without having some sort of interest in it. Plus, we made some adaptations and changes as the kids worked on these problems. What I encourage teachers to do is to come up with their own projects, to create problems for their students that will be meaningful to them.

6

But What Do They Know?

Assessment

David is writing about his progress in the following areas:

Challenging Myself: I think I have been challenging myself at descriptive writing. I used to not have very descriptive writing, now I do.

Independence: When I first came into this room I would always ask what to do next. Now I just do everything on my own.

Confidence: Right now I am pretty confident. I really don't think I have got more confident.

As I was sitting uncomfortably in my cramped seat, flying from Portland, Maine, to Portland, Oregon, after a conference in May 1994, I turned to Ruth Hubbard and asked, "How can I write a chapter on assessment? I don't do any." She looked at me and shook her head and laughed, as she often does in reaction to the things I say. She reminded me of something Larry, an eight-year-old, had said to me last year. He had just moved into our classroom a few months before from a very traditional classroom. I asked him how reading was different in our room than in his other room. He looked at me smiling and said, "We don't have to do reading in your room." He was obviously extremely excited by this thought. I, on the other hand, was quite puzzled. "Well, Larry," I asked him, "What are you doing with that book?" He looked at the book and then looked back up at me. "I'm reading. We're not *doing* reading."

Later, when he again moved into a very traditional environment, he told me during a phone conversation that now he had to *do* math. I suppose since we don't have math workbooks or a special "math time," new kids from a more traditional curriculum don't think we do it.

Ruth and I generated a long list of assessment and evaluation strategies that I do use in my classroom. Just because something doesn't have a label attached to it, doesn't mean you aren't doing it. The children are reading, writing, and *experiencing* math all day long, and I am assessing them all day long. Yet, not until I sat down and began listing what I was doing, did I realize just how much I do, and how often I do it.

EVERYDAY ASSESSMENT

Every time I talk to the children I am learning about them. I like the words "learning about" much more than I like "assessing." I learn about my children. I get to know them. I want to know *what* they know. I want to know *how* they know. Isn't that what assessment is all about—learning what children know? When I ask a six-year-old to tell me about her weekend, I am learning how this child tells a story. I learn if she can tell a story, if the story makes sense—is there a beginning, a middle, and an end? I am learning what interests the child, what the child talks about, and what is important to the child, and I am learning more about the child. All this from one small question. Observation and listening are the most important strategies I use for learning about the children in my class.

As Carly was presenting her Journey Problem journal, she came to a part in which she needed to mention what countries she had traveled through. She said, "We went through Asia, Europe, and Africa." Now, because I know Carly so well, I could ask the class the following question: "Did Carly just share what countries she traveled through?" Someone noticed her mistake and said, "No."

"Do you see that Carly?" I asked her. I watched her glance over her journal. She looked up and smiled. "Oh, I looked at the wrong line. These are the continents. The next ones I share will be the countries." That was a quick on-the-spot assessment. I knew that Carly knew the difference between countries and continents, so by asking her to see her mix-up, I could listen to her response and watch her face. I would have been able to tell if she was confused by the expression on her face. I didn't need to give her a test or assign page after page of geography worksheets to find out what she knew about countries and continents. And I knew she'd be comfortable being put on the spot like that. I could not put Megan or Alissa on the spot like that. If I had a similar question for them, I would pull them aside later.

I use these on-the-spot assessments often. As we sat on the grass in front of the school during Quiet Writing one afternoon, after we had finished sharing but before I wanted to go back inside, I asked everyone to find one thing and then another thing that was about four times as big as the first thing. The children went off for about three minutes and then we met back in a circle. What they found was interesting but even more so how they "proved" the bigger item was four times bigger. Clearly, some of the children needed practice estimating, some needed practice measuring accurately, and some had a fairly precise sense of "times-bigger."

The facial expressions of children help me understand the "sense" they have of particular concepts. Watch your students' faces one day as you question them about a concept. I have seen looks anywhere from extreme confidence to total bewilderment. These expressions help me to know when I need to back off or when I need to step in and help a child with a concept they find confusing.

I find myself constantly assessing during Writing and Reading Workshop. Through conferences, I know what a child knows and what a child needs to work on. Dave, who has an uncanny love for writing, was working on a piece that had a section of dialogue. I asked him if he knew what he needs when he writes dialogue.

"Oh yeah, these little things, quotes, right? But I never know where to put 'em." So I showed him. Days later, during another conference with Dave, after he had finished reading his story to me I concentrated on how he was using quotes. I also find it easy during writing conferences to see the progress the child has made since our last conference. When I notice a skill or concept a child has been consistently using and understanding, I will record that progress on their progress wheels.

PROGRESS WHEELS

The year I taught in England, I was introduced to the National Curriculum (NC). The teachers in my school were trying to understand this new curriculum, not to mention all the new record-keeping sheets. I had never seen so much paperwork. I had seen an example of some sort of recording system in an article or book I

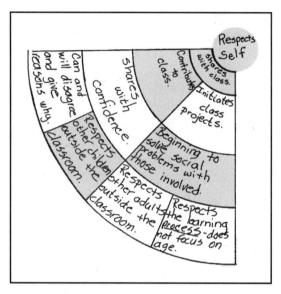

FIGURE 20a Portion of a shaded progress wheel.

was reading. It was in the shape of a wheel and looked very organized. I decided to try to put the Reading, Writing, Speaking, and Listening parts of the NC onto such a recording wheel to make it easier to keep track of the children's progress. I remember it as being quite an intense job. I also helped to create a wheel for the Maths NC. The staff seemed to like using this record-keeping strategy.

When I was back in the States and beginning my teaching at my present school, I decided to make progress wheels for my own personal record-keeping system. I created one for reading and writing. These wheels were very useful to me that first year. I was able to explain them easily to parents, who appreciated the fact that the wheels were so visual. I like the fact that the wheels are not linear, since I look at children as "scattered" learners. As Figure 20a shows, it is easy to see that these wheels are not linear continuums. Children don't learn in neat, straight lines.

The following year I updated the wheels a bit, condensing them more, yet by June I realized that I wasn't really using them as often as I needed to. When I'm not using a tool, I either don't need it anymore, or it is time to update and change it. Last summer I spent time updating the wheels so they would be more useful to me.

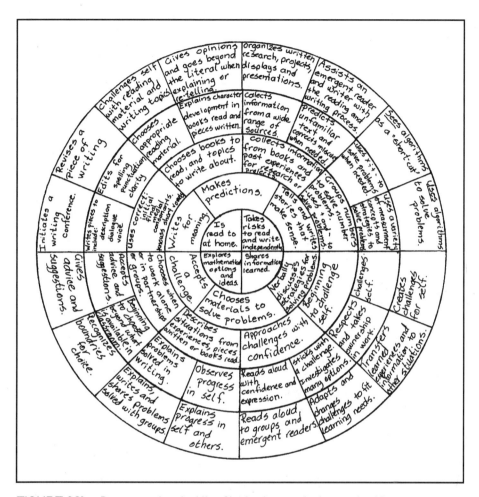

FIGURE 20b Progress wheel of the Student as an Independent Learner.

I thought a lot about what I would consider important as I ventured into this class of first-, second-, and third-grade children. I knew I did not want to separate them into grade levels. I *couldn't* separate them into grade levels! I made a list of all of the qualities I watch in children as they progress over time. I knew that choice, challenge, independence, and respect were important to me. After I had listed the skills that I thought would be of help to me, I made some lists. What I discovered in the lists was a common theme and consistency. Finally I came up with the two topic headings I use on the most recent wheels, *Progress as an Independent Learner* and *Progress as a Community Learner* (see Figures 20b and 20c).

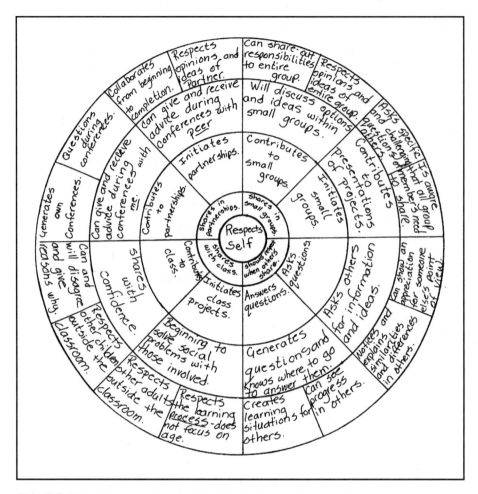

FIGURE 20c Progress wheel of the Student as a Community Learner.

When I was showing the progress wheels to Ruth, she told me she could actually use parts of them for her graduate students. I think that is probably true. There are sections that I wish all adults could shade in, especially the section under Community Learner that says, *can show an appreciation for someone else's point of view.*

I condensed the content areas significantly. I have found that I just don't need to know every writing skill I had listed on the old wheels. All the emergent writing stages on the original wheels seemed trivial. I replaced these sections with *Writes for meaning.* That gives me the same information in less space.

I also took out all the specific math skills. It matters less to me that a child *knows* his math facts to 10 or 20 than how a child *uses* math facts. I added two sections about algorithms: *Sees algorithms as a "shortcut"* and *Uses algorithms to solve problems.* I have noticed that at a certain point, children begin to see algorithms as a shortcut in solving problems. They begin to realize that they don't need to use cubes or tens strips all the time. That is an important realization, so I added it into the wheel. When children begin to use algorithms consistently to solve problems, I know they have truly internalized the concept. Because we don't use math workbooks or any commercial math program, this is a vital observation for my records.

The community progress wheel is also a very important and essential record-keeping tool for me. Since I honor a sense of community so strongly, I need a way to record how the children progress as community members. I added a number of comments about respect. No child, or adult, can be an effective community member without respect. And the core of respecting others is respecting oneself, which is why I put *respects self* at the center of the wheel.

These progress wheels have proven themselves effective record-keeping tools this year. I don't feel an overwhelming desire to change them, but I'll probably add or take away comments as I need to. I don't shade these in every day or even every month. I usually do it just before conferences or reporting time, or whenever I feel I need to look more closely at a child's progress. Each child has a wheel, which I keep in one of their portfolios.

Some parents have asked me, "What now?" when their child's wheels have been completely filled in. I don't see these wheels as learning *goals*, I use them more for observing learning *strategies.* For these children, this kind of record-keeping might have outlived its usefulness to me, and we need to expand further on those strategies.

"AUTHENTIC" ASSESSMENT

What could tell a teacher more about a child than an assessment that really *means* something? That sounds so simple, but assessment should be simple. Authentic assessments show what a child *knows.* I don't use assessment to discover what a child does not know. Standardized tests do that quite nicely! They are of no use to me.

Authentic assessments force me to look more at the process and less at the product. These assessments should not be standardized in any way, such as the

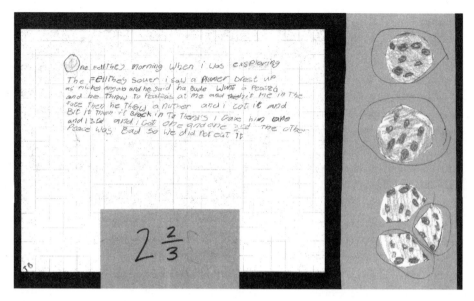

FIGURE 21   JB's fraction problem solution.

reading assessments the whole second grade does, or spelling assessments for the first grade. I have seen these types of assessments used in schools, but to me there is no difference between them and standardized testing. Neither focuses on *process,* and those little tests are not in keeping with what we know today about good child-centered practice.

A fraction problem turned out to be an authentic assessment that I hadn't intended as an assessment. I discovered it after the children had completed the assignment. I asked the kids to pick a card with a fraction written on it. Then I asked them to do two things with the fraction they had picked:

1. Show the fraction using a picture.
2. Write a story explaining the fraction.

It was clear to me from their response to this problem what each child knew about fractions on both a concrete and an abstract level. I know, for example, that JB has a clear sense of numerical fractions and abstract fractions (see Figure 21). He not only understands the concept of mixed fractions, but his written explanation showed that he could find a different way to see the fraction 2⅔. When I questioned him about his written answer, he said, "Well, when I

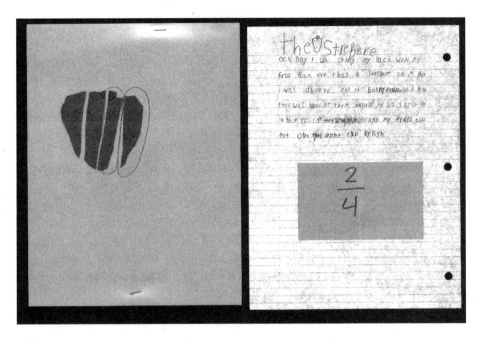

FIGURE 22   Kyle's picture and response to a fraction problem.

put the picture down, I noticed another way to say 2⅔. It's 1 and 1⅓ and ⅓ left over. So I decided to write about that instead." He not only challenged himself, but he used what he knew about fractions to look at this one in a new way.

I know that Kyle has a clear sense of numerical fractions but is not yet ready to fully understand fractions abstractly (see Figure 22). He was quick to draw and cut the picture of the strawberry. He knew that the bottom number meant "how many in all" and that the top number meant "how many to show," but watching him write his story was very different. He was obviously confused. His writing was actually pretty accurate, but he was very unsure of his answer when it came time to share his problem and answer questions from the class.

Anna is still learning to understand fractions numerically and with pictures (see Figure 23). She is learning to represent fractions pictorially. When she picked her fraction card, she took it to a table and sat staring at it for a long time. She saw Kyle making a strawberry and I noticed that she began making a strawberry too. When she had completed cutting out the picture, I walked over to her.

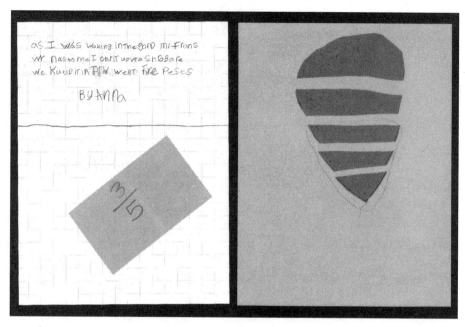

As I was woking in the gord mifrons wr nastome I cnrit uovra shobale we kuub it in AF weer fire pests

BY Anna

3/5

FIGURE 23 Anna's solution to a fraction problem.

"Okay, Anna," I said, "You have a strawberry. What do you need to do to the strawberry now?"

"Cut it up?"

"Yep. How many pieces do you need to cut it into?"

"Three?" she asked.

"Good guess! What does the 3 mean in ⅗?"

"How many in all?" I noticed that all of Anna's answers were asked as questions. This was significant in terms of her confidence with this concept.

"Try again."

"Oh, yeah. The top number is how many you take and the bottom number is how many in all, right?"

"What do you think?"

"I think yes. So the 5 is how many pieces to cut. I'll cut my strawberry into five pieces and circle three pieces." Without this sort of questioning, she would have been confused and frustrated. Through questioning and reinforcement, she became very confident about her final answer.

Although this sort of questioning was appropriate for Anna, it wouldn't have been for Kyle. He needed to take time to experiment with his knowledge, and he was comfortable doing so. These three samples might seem to indicate that these children have a clear numerical and abstract concept of fractions. Yet obviously not all of them do. The reason I call this an *authentic* assessment is that this problem shows me where each child is. Had I given the kids a pencil and paper test that asked them to circle the correct fraction or to shade in the numerical fraction shown, I would not have learned what I did about how much the children do know, how they know it, and what they need to know.

The other point is that I don't always look for the correct answer. I look for the process a child goes through to find the answer to a problem. Even though Anna finally did understand what she was doing, her process was different from that of Kyle and JB, and theirs were different from everyone else in the class. Anna's explanation at the end of my questioning made it clear to her that she did understand what she was doing. As Kyle was sharing, he was aware that his written explanation confused him. He knew he understood the picture, but he also knew he needed to work more on fraction stories. JB was able to challenge himself to go further and test out his knowledge.

I remember the first time Danny did a play that made sense. That too was a form of authentic assessment. Danny, a first grader, acquired oral language at age six. I know he is beginning to develop an understanding of story in terms of beginning, middle, and ending. He made up and performed a short play in which he had these three elements. Every time I see children using or making up new spelling strategies to help them spell, I list those strategies as authentic assessments. Rachel, for example, writes lists for checking her spelling all the time. And when a child moves from writing with only consonant sounds to adding short vowels, I know that child has made a huge step in his writing progress.

Before conferences I borrowed an idea from Allyn Snider. I wrote five addition problems ranging in difficulty from an addition fact to a three-digit problem on a piece of paper. I told the children to choose the one they felt was right for them, solve it, and write about how they solved it. This was a wonderful assessment of many things besides whether or not the children could add. I observed how independent children were in solving the problem, how—and if—they would challenge themselves, and how detailed their writing was.

Chuck chose to do the first problem (see Figure 24a). He wrote that he solved it using unifix cubes. Chuck is a second grader and knowing that cubes were available to him was a huge step for him. He also tried to challenge him-

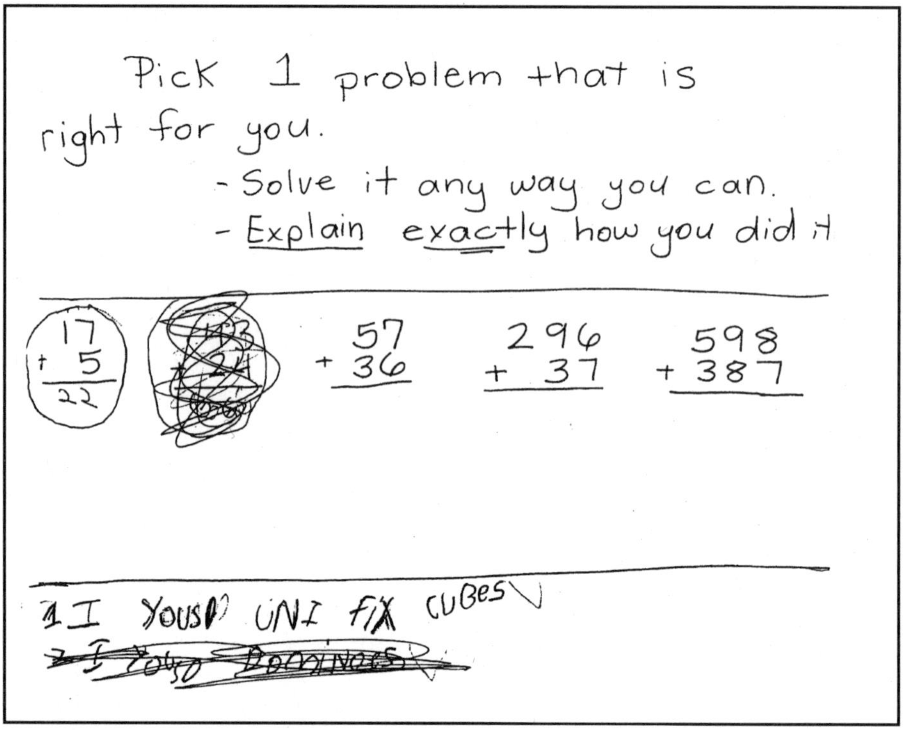

Pick 1 problem that is
right for you.
    - Solve it any way you can.
    - Explain exactly how you did it

$$\begin{array}{r} 17 \\ + 5 \\ \hline 22 \end{array}$$ $$\begin{array}{r} 57 \\ + 36 \\ \hline \end{array}$$ $$\begin{array}{r} 296 \\ + 37 \\ \hline \end{array}$$ $$\begin{array}{r} 598 \\ + 387 \\ \hline \end{array}$$

1 I yousd UNI fix cubes

FIGURE 24a Chuck works out the first problem.

self by doing the second problem. From his scratch out, it would seem that he felt it was too difficult for him to solve. He then decided to try one that would be better for him. Megan also chose the first problem, but she solved it very differently. She wrote, "I took 17 in my head and added 5 with my fingers." She understands the concept of counting on, yet she didn't need cubes to solve this. She too wanted to try the second problem but didn't begin to try it as Chuck had. She has much less confidence than Chuck, so this seemed right for Megan. Alissa was becoming more comfortable using ten strips. She even drew a picture of what the strips looked like when she had added the two numbers together. The fact that she doesn't need cubes but isn't yet ready to add large numbers without ten strips is a significant insight into Alissa's progress. When she becomes more confident using the strips, I can begin to have her record on paper just how the ten strips work.

Chris also used counting, but he wanted to challenge himself by solving the third problem. He started with 57 and then added the 36 to come up with

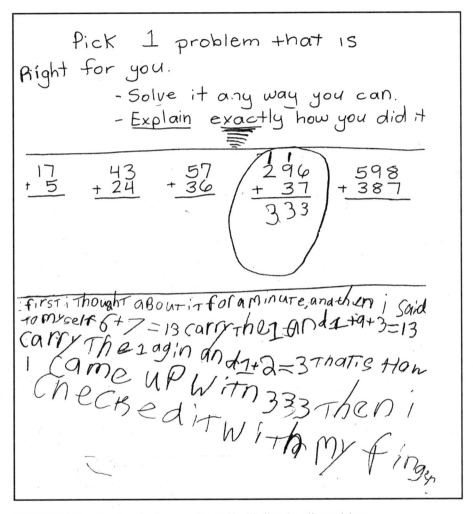

FIGURE 24b Tessia challenges herself with the fourth problem.

his answer. Tessia also challenged herself with the problem (see Figure 24b). Her writing explains clearly that she can *do* an algorithm, although I would question her *understanding* of it. When she wrote, "I carried the 1," I would question her to see if she understands that what she is carrying is actually a 10, not a 1. Josh understands this algorithm. He can solve it mathematically and write about how he solves it.

The importance of this quick assessment wasn't the accuracy of the answers. It was the children's explanations of how they solved the problem.

Chuck and Megan both solved the same problem, but their strategies were quite different. When I assess and evaluate, I tend to focus more on strategy than on accuracy.

Yet, sometimes I do want to check accuracy and how much a child has learned or internalized. When we begin a topic or research project, I will ask the children to write down everything they know about the topic. For example, when we studied space a year ago, before we even began our study, I asked the kids to write down everything they knew about space. Some kids wrote, "I know nothing," and others wrote that they knew the sun and the moon and the stars are in space. I dated these and saved them. Then, at the end of the study, I again asked the kids to write everything they knew about space. This was a wonderful assessment of how much the kids had learned. I dated these papers, stapled them to the first one the kids had written, and put them into their portfolios.

PORTFOLIOS

I see *portfolio* as another term on its way to "term hell." There are two different kinds of portfolio. One is Portfolio Assessment, and the other is the Working Portfolio. *Portfolio Assessment* is a collection of the child's best work gathered together for the sole purpose of assessment. *Working Portfolios* are collections of work the child does all year. I use these two types of portfolios for my children as well as one other.

1. Portfolio of Assessments (PA): This is a portfolio of authentic assessments I might give the child throughout the year. In this portfolio I might also include observations and the progress wheels. This portfolio is a collection of work I have specifically chosen for assessing that child. I use this collection not simply as a collection of the child's work but for a more critical look at the child. This is where the child and I may choose to put a "best piece" of work.

2. The Working Portfolios (WP): These portfolios are collections of the child's work. The kids file their own work in four folders: writing, math, projects, and art. Their writing drafts are filed in their writing folders, which contain every piece of writing the child has done during Writing Workshop. This is also a great way to observe writing progress quickly. The math portfolio works the same way, as does the project portfolio, except for one difference: if a project or

problem is too large to fit inside the folder, I ask the child to write about what they have done and put that writing into the portfolio. I have also taken pictures of projects to go into these portfolios, but film and processing tends to get expensive, so I have found that the written explanation is sufficient. The art portfolios hold all the art work the child has done during art workshop.

These ever-growing files contain all the work the child has done during the year. Instead of sending work home, I ask the kids to keep it in these Working Portfolios so we can follow their progress by comparing their work from different parts of the school year.

3. The Pass-On Portfolio (PO): This is the portfolio that is to be passed on to the child's next teacher. (Some teachers call these *cumulative portfolios*.) It serves as a sample of work that clearly shows where the child began, how far the child came, and where the child needs to go. This is where samples of writing that show progress should be included. I do not use PO Portfolios as an assessment tool for the next teacher. They are not a judgment piece, but rather a sample of work a new teacher can look at to get a *feel* for the child. These portfolios should be quite small, since no teacher will, or will want to, shuffle through a huge packet of work for twenty-six children. They should also be selective, showing a piece of writing that demonstrates the child's knowledge of the writing process, an authentic math assessment, an evaluation by the child, and so on. I also use these portfolios as the carriers of my notes and/or record-keeping on the child. (I remove the progress wheel from the PA portfolio and stick it into the PO portfolio.)

In a PO portfolio I like to include samples of writing that show children's progress and their knowledge of the writing process. This could include one from the beginning of the year and one from the end of the year. I include a short explanation about why the pieces were included. The child also does this. Some teachers use spelling assessments as progress, others use spelling as part of the writing process. Both are valid forms of *spelling* assessment but not of writing assessment! Two or three samples of authentic assessments should be included. Knowing that a child received 83 percent on a math test would be of no help to me! Knowing what a child knows about a concept would be. Teachers often say, "But I don't know what to include." I advise them to decide on a few items that show the child's learning. Of course it is difficult to include a piece of work on all mathematical concepts. Most teachers don't want to see that. I included the fraction assessment in some of my students' portfolios.

I see teachers trying to use all of these portfolios at once. It helps to be clear on what you are saving, what needs to go to the child, and what needs to be passed on to the next teacher. In some cases, I find a piece of work that will fit into all of these portfolios, and the child and I might decide together where it belongs.

PA is a tool I use to keep track of what the child knows. It is easy to look into this portfolio and see what a child understands about a particular concept. As I explained to the kids, the fraction problem I gave them might be something I would put into this portfolio. This was not a "right/wrong" type of assessment. It simply showed me what the children knew about fractions.

I *don't* think continuity in PO portfolios is all that crucial. All portfolios can and should be different: all children are different and their work should look different. Portfolios should respect the individuality of the child.

RUBRICS

Rubric. This is a word I had never even heard of until a few years ago. Now it seems as if everyone is using it. What concerns me about rubrics is that they are often used in a hierarchy, and when they are, I don't see much difference between a rubric and a grade. The ones I have seen used by other teachers are on scales of one to five or something of that sort. But I can't compare children like that, even if the children create their own rubrics. I don't want them to think they can judge people or themselves in terms of a scale or grading system.

Another concern I have with rubrics as they are typically used is that they seem to put a cap on the expectations for a project. They may make it easy for a child to do all the requirements, but I wonder how much a child would challenge herself.

EXPECTATIONS

I have very high expectations of all of my students. I expect them to go beyond what is expected of them. I expect them to challenge themselves, I expect them to challenge each other, and I expect them to surprise me with what they are capable of doing.

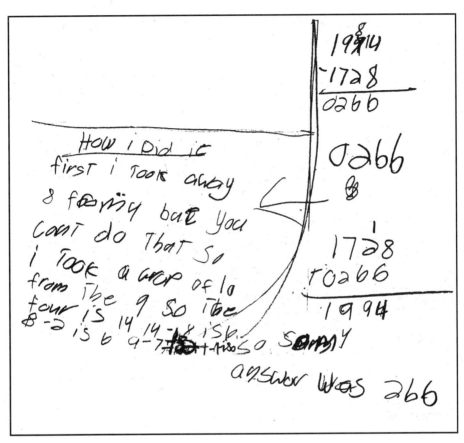

FIGURE 25a   JB creates a more challenging problem for himself.

I gave the children a small problem when we were studying the history of our island. It went like this:

> Choose any date from your island family tree. Figure out how long ago that was from 1994. Explain how you did it.

JB came to me with his problem. I noticed several problems on his paper and asked him why he did two. He told me that the first date he chose was easy; it didn't require any borrowing, so he wanted to do a more challenging one. Then he checked his answers by addition (see Figure 25a). Kyle decided to pick 1786 to take away from 1994. I knew he did not know how to do an algorithm

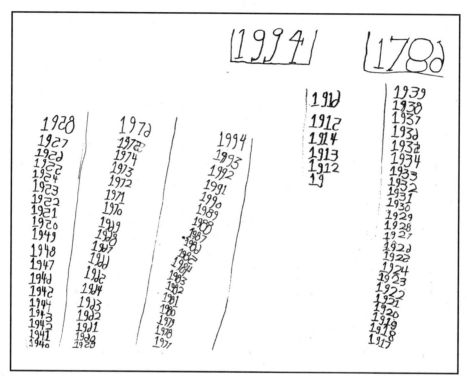

FIGURE 25b Kyle's strategy to solve a complex problem.

for subtracting such high numbers, but because he was familiar with trying to solve such complex problems, off he went to try and figure out a way to do it. He began with 1994 and proceeded to count backwards, writing down the dates as he went (see Figure 25b). He didn't plan on stopping until he reached 1786! Then, he took a break from writing numbers to come and listen to Kiersten's explanation of how she solved the problem.

"Well, I got the orange things (3-D plastic place value cubes, mats, strips, and units). I took the big cube 'cause that's a thousand. Then I got nine mats 'cause they're hundreds. Then I got nine strips 'cause they're tens. Then I got four little ones for the ones. That made 1994. Then I drew pictures for the orange things. I drew a big box for the thousand. Then I drew smaller boxes for the hundreds and long boxes for the tens and tiny boxes for the ones. Then I shaded what I needed to take away. That's all I did."

"Kiersten, can you tell us what you shaded?"

FIGURE 25c Kiersten finds the solution for 1994 − 1790.

"Okay. I shaded the whole big box 'cause I needed to take away a thousand. Then I shaded seven hundreds, then nine tens and zero ones."

"And what was your final answer?"

"Um. Twenty-four? No, I mean two hundred and four."

"Why did you say twenty-four?"

"Because it was twenty and then four but when I looked at the picture, there was two hundred and then four little ones" (see Figure 25c).

Kyle went back and tried the problem Kiersten's way, as did many of the children.

"Hey Jill, it works! That's fun, but can I still finish doing my way too?"

These children clearly know that there is no cap on expectation. They know they can challenge themselves as far as they want to go.

It's also interesting to observe what the children choose to challenge themselves with. Their writing is easy to assess through observation. Their drafts are strictly drafts—messy and in-process. Yet when I ask them to write a letter to their seventh-grade pen pals, they do it carefully. I know the difference between writing nonfiction prose and writing a letter to my friend. Children know this too. I still have high expectations for my students as they draft, but it isn't about neatness. I expect them to write exciting leads and to fill their piece with description and dialogue and interesting characters.

Before I assess the children, I ask myself what my expectation is in terms of the experience I am assessing. *Every* experience has a different expectation.

CONFERENCES

The children also do many assessments on their own or with other children. Every question they ask during our share times is an assessment. Kyle asks incredibly detailed questions. He listens so intently and his questions are always very specific. How children answer questions is also an important assessing tool.

Besides question and answer, the children also assess themselves more formally. At my school, we schedule parent conferences twice a year. I hold student-led conferences in which the children accompany their parents to their own conference and present work from their portfolios. For the March conferences with parents, I decided to have the children become more involved. I have found that most of the children are very quiet and reluctant to speak up at their conferences. So I gave each student a folder and asked them to do two things to get ready for their conferences. On the left side of the folder, I had attached a sheet that asked about their progress. I wanted to know how the kids felt they had progressed in the following areas: challenging yourself, independence, confidence, reading, writing, math, and projects. Instead of making the academic areas the focus, I let challenge, independence, and confidence be the main focus. The written responses were very honest and informative. For young children, focusing on academic progress seems to be very difficult.

On the right side of the folder was a list of the work I asked the kids to collect for their conference portfolio. The list included a piece of writing that shows description, editing, and progress from the beginning of the year; a piece of research; a favorite book; math samples that include one problem and something showing addition, subtraction, multiplication, or division; a piece of art; and a project.

As with most portfolios, space is a problem. Kiersten wanted to put in her big project from her holiday research, but it wouldn't fit. This was true for all of the projects. I told the kids that if they wanted to include something in their conference portfolio that couldn't fit or wasn't at school anymore, they had to write about it. This turned out to be a great idea because it enabled the children to talk more during their conferences. I have also taken pictures of some of the larger projects. I glue the picture on a piece of paper and let the kids write about the picture.

When the kids came in with their parents for their conference, they were in charge. I was there to inform, add more explanation, answer questions, and ask questions. These were the most informative and successful conferences I have had.

Many teachers are experimenting with student-led conferences and want to learn more about them. Terri Austin, a teacher researcher from Alaska, has written *Changing the View*, a book about a research project dealing with this topic.

7

The Mainland:
The Larger Community

Over the years, as I have presented at conferences and held workshops on various topics, I have noticed that similar questions seem to arise during the question and answer time. Those same questions also come up when visitors come to my classroom. In this chapter, I want to answer some of the more frequently asked questions.

I consider the parents of the children in my class a part of my "larger community." It has been just as wonderful for me to see them grow and change over the years as it has watching their children. I have asked some parents to consider a number of questions, and they have graciously agreed to answer them. So, the second half of this chapter is devoted to the parents of children who have been in my class.

COMMONLY ASKED QUESTIONS

How do you prepare your students for the fourth-grade teacher? This question always startles me. Am I *supposed* to be preparing children for the next teacher? Is that what education is all about? Is that how life works? I remember answering that question at a conference by comparing it to something in real life. I asked the audience if I should be getting *prepared* to give birth because sometime in my future I may want to. The answer seems a bit silly now, but I still believe there are some parallels. Children don't need to be prepared to go on to a different teacher. They need to be prepared to move on in their education, prepared in the sense that they will be able to accept new challenges. I don't feel I need to prepare children for a teacher they may have in the future who might have different beliefs than I do. What they need is the best their present teacher can offer them. I hope my students take with them to their next teacher a sense of confidence and independence, and an ability to challenge themselves and take risks. It's funny that no one ever asks, "Who has prepared the children for *you*?" I often get new second-grade children who are totally lost the first month of school. They have no idea how to chose a book by themselves. They have no idea how to write something without a topic. They have no idea how to explain how they have solved a math problem. They don't know how to work respectfully in a group. Yet, over time, they learn these skills, which I value and want them to value. Children who have gone into fourth-grade rooms that give spelling tests and fact worksheets have come to me to complain the first few weeks of school, but soon enough they just get used to it. No, I don't prepare them to take a spelling test or do a fact worksheet, but I have tried to prepare them to understand what to do with the information on a spelling test or a fact worksheet. I want them to be life-long learners, questioning and analyzing what is asked of them.

Since you don't do math fact worksheets or seem to have the kids memorize their facts, how will they know them when they leave your class? That question, too, surprises me, especially after an hour-long presentation of my math program! But still, it comes up, so I assume it's on many teachers' minds. One day I decided to pose it to the children as a problem. I asked them to think about what they would do if someone came walking into the room right this minute and demanded that they prove they know their math facts. Off they went to do this. Dave, a second grader, proved he knew his multiplication facts of two. He made a Civil War battle field with soldiers walking to a hillside. Each time, the group picked up two more soldiers. He wrote the fact on top of each group. Kiersten, a first grader, proved she knew her addition facts to 10 by using unifix cubes and drawing squares on a huge piece of white paper. When she was finished, she wrote the sum underneath each tower she had drawn, leaving the unifix towers next to what she had drawn. Zack, a third grader, proved he knew his multiplication facts of 9 by using graph paper. He marked off nine squares each time and wrote the answer down next to the line of squares. He also noticed a pattern: the answers for the nine facts also went backwards.

What this little problem, or experiment, showed me was that, not only did the children know their facts, but they could visualize them with pictures, graphs, and charts. They could also explain the patterns of the facts they were solving. They could also come up with extremely creative ways to do this totally independently. They knew *much* more than just what the answer was on a fact sheet. The children in the class *use* math facts every day. I don't need to test them on whether they know them. They wouldn't be able to solve some of the complex problems they do without this knowledge. Just as children will learn the sounds for the letters by using them, experimenting, and practicing them constantly during Writing Workshop, so children will learn their math facts by using them, experimenting with them, and practicing them during a Math Workshop.

How do your kids do on standardized tests?   I don't believe that standardized tests really show what a child *can* do, I think standardized tests show what a child *can't* do. In my school district, we test children from third grade on up. My kids have typically done quite well on these tests, but they find them boring and "stupid." I remember the questions they had as they were taking one of the state tests:

"I don't get this! There are no right answers. What should I mark?"

"These stories aren't very interesting! There's no description."

"How come we don't have to explain how we solved these math problems?"

I learned much more from those questions than I did from the scores on these tests. Children who are able to read quickly do well on the reading section, but I don't always see those children as the most critical readers. Children who are quick at adding up sums, solving math facts, and using standard algorithms do well on the math section, but children who use different strategies that take time do not do as well because of the time restraints.

So, how do my kids do on these tests? To tell you the truth, I rarely pay attention to them. I did go back and check in order to respond to this question, and the third graders did quite well. I wasn't surprised. And the kids who didn't get a "high score" didn't surprise me either. I didn't learn anything new from these tests. I always worry about giving the tests, fearing that if the children do poorly it will reflect on my teaching. I have come to relax a bit more and trust my own knowledge of what the kids can do.

What about all the slow kids and the kids who need to go to Chapter 1? How do they do in your room? I don't see children as "slow." I don't see children at age seven needing extra reading help because they can't read yet. I don't look at children in terms of an arbitrary grade or age level. I look at children as individual learners who *all* learn at different rates. I don't refer children to special reading services. Period. I feel that with the support I give, and the way my program is set up to look at where a child starts, I can best serve all the children in my class. I am confident enough in my program that the children will progress. *All* children progress, some slower than others, but is that bad? Is that a problem?

Because I don't refer children and I have a class of respected and respectful children, I am often accused of having a "hand-picked" class, a class of all the "smart" kids. I actually had one teacher believe that I interviewed children before they were allowed into my room! I used to take comments like those as compliments to my program. Now, I just look at them as showing a lack of understanding on the part of the person making the comments.

I look at the potential in all of my children, not the deficits. It seems as if reading is the only determination in the lower grades of whether or not a child is "slow" or "gifted." Anna, a third-grade girl this year, who is still finding reading a struggle, has the most gifted sense of social justice I have ever seen. But look at what we value in schools: most young children are referred to special services or to gifted education programs on the basis of reading test scores.

I adapt my programs for the children; I don't expect them to adapt to my program.

Your kids seem to have such long attention spans! My kids could never sit still that long and listen. This is a common observation from visitors. It never even occurred to me to look at attention span, or "on-task" behavior, until people started commenting on it. I just take it for granted. Why wouldn't the whole group *want* to listen to others when they share? And for those who don't, the rest of the class will remind them how rude it is to talk when someone else is sharing. (They are much harder on each other than I am.)

When children are interested and have ownership of what they are doing, they listen. And they work. If I had twenty-seven desks and asked the kids to do page after page of worksheets, never letting them move around the room, yes, they would rebel! And so they should. I can't sit at a desk or a table for more than fifteen minutes at a time without getting squirmy. How can I expect an eight-year-old to do so? But, if I were in a circle of my favorite authors listening to them read their work, I could sit for hours. The kids' favorite authors are each other. They can sit for long periods of time listening to each other read stories.

A big buzz word in the "disorder" category is Attention Deficit (Hyperactivity) Disorder, AD(H)D. I've never had a child with this disorder. I think it's because I don't have my kids sit for long periods of time. That's not to say I don't believe *some* children actually have AD(H)D. But the percentage is far less than the percentage of children who are referred for it. I have heard of only one child in my fourteen years of teaching that sounds as if he truly has an attention disorder. Two of my friends have taught him, and in different school settings.

If kids aren't paying attention or are "off-task," think about what they are being asked to listen to, or what the "task" is first.

What happens when a substitute comes into your room? I try to find a substitute I can call throughout the year when I know I will be away from the classroom. I ask that sub to come into my room at the beginning of the year to get to know the class. In the past, I have been able to use former interns.

The other thing I have found helpful for subs is to have the kids plan for the days when I am gone. We all sit down together and they plan the day. I record the name of the child who wants to be responsible for that part of the day. For instance, they usually want to do Writing Workshop in the afternoons. We write down the times and the name of a student the sub can talk to if she has any questions. This works well for the days I know I am going to be gone. Since the kids have done the planning, they are prepared.

When I am out with an illness and the kids don't know I will be gone, this kind of planning doesn't work. The regular sub knows what to do and how the day is structured. For the times I can't get my usual sub, I have the new sub call me in the morning so I can talk about the class and what to do during the day. I like to have subs do most of their own planning. I'd rather they do what they feel comfortable with than have them try to do something I want them to do and have an awful day. Usually, the subs I have had love doing some sort of art activity or science thing. It is so much more beneficial for subs to do what they are interested in. The kids seem to have better days and the sub must feel more in control.

The kids are so independent and know the routine so well, I rarely have trouble when they have a sub. Of course, there are always those kids who have a hard time with any kind of change, but I usually talk to the sub about those particular children so she can talk to them and reassure them that I will be back.

My school wants to start blended (multi-aged) classrooms, but parents are scared that the older kids won't be challenged. That's a problem, but it is a problem not only for multi-aged rooms but for straight grade rooms as well. If parents don't feel that their child will be challenged in a blended class, what made them feel they were being challenged in a straight grade class?

I remind parents about the range of levels in a straight grade classroom. I explain that every child is challenged. There is no difference in a multi-aged classroom, unless the teacher doesn't believe in them. I don't think teachers should be forced to teach something they don't believe in. If they do, the class will end up being a split class with the third graders doing one thing and the fourth graders doing another.

Multi-aged classrooms, especially those like mine, with a three- or four-year age span, force teachers to look at children as individuals. How could I possibly give a spelling test to my entire class? I challenge each child, not just the ones at the "top" or the oldest. This means finding what is just beyond what a child finds easy, and that is different for every child. I believe straight grades need to do that just as much as multi-aged classes.

I don't look at children as "age level" or "grade level." I simply look at them as children.

Which professional books have you found particularly helpful? Here's a list of the books I've found most helpful:

In the Middle: Writing, Reading, and Learning with Adolescents by Nancie Atwell.

Changing the View: Student-led Parent Conferences by Terri Austin.

About Teaching Mathematics by Marilyn Burns.

Writing to Learn Mathematics by Joan Countryman.

Picturing Learning: Artists and Writers in the Classroom by Karen Ernst.

What's Whole in Whole Language? by Kenneth S. Goodman.

Writing: Children and Teachers at Work by Donald H. Graves.

Breaking Ground: Teachers Relate Reading and Writing in the Elementary School by Jane Hansen, Thomas Newkirk, and Donald H. Graves.

A Workshop of the Possible by Ruth Hubbard.

Literacy in Process: The Heinemann Reader by Ruth Hubbard, and Brenda M. Power.

Learning Denied by Denny Taylor.

You Kan Red This! Spelling and Punctuation for Whole Language Classrooms, K-6 by Sandra Wilde.

I highly recommend any and all of those books. There are dozens of others I have read and enjoyed, but those listed have been particularly helpful to me.

I have also given Ken Goodman's *What's Whole in Whole Language* to parents to read. It is an easy-to-follow book that parents have found very helpful. I have also given parents articles from *Breaking Ground* and *Literacy in Process* to read. The more parents are educated, the more they understand why the room works the way it does. I am not shy about sharing current research or interesting articles and books with them.

PARENTS

Many people also ask me how new parents react when they enter my classroom. They react in a variety of ways. Parents of first graders who are familiar with my room are extremely supportive and thankful that their children are in the class. Parents of first graders who were randomly placed in the room have interesting reactions. One parent walked into the room with her incoming first-grade son in August to meet me before school began. She looked around the room and then looked at me with a worried expression on her face. "Where are the desks?" That same parent is now explaining the dynamics of the room to other parents. She was helped by the more experienced parents who'd already had children in my classroom for two or three years. I encourage new parents to talk with other parents about any concerns or questions they might have. A common question new parents ask other parents is, "What about spelling tests? How do the kids learn how to spell?" Parents whose children have gone through the program are very articulate and knowledgeable in answering that question.

When questions persist, or when I sense that a parent is confused or concerned about something, I will approach the parent and suggest a conference. It's funny that most of the concerns new parents have are about spelling and math facts. Yet when they begin to observe the amount of self-confidence and independence, and the love for learning their child is gaining, they begin to realize how the smaller pieces fit into the more global picture. I often hear parents explaining the importance of a holistic learning environment to other parents.

I made up a short questionnaire about specifics of the classroom environment and how their children have approached learning because of that environment. I gave it to parents who currently have children in my room and to parents whose child has been in my class in the past. There were some commonalties in many of the responses. For instance, one of the questions I asked the parents to comment on was how their thinking has changed about *how* children learn as a result of having their child in my classroom. Almost everyone wrote that they learned how vital process was, not just product. One parent wrote, "The interaction between the children is a motivation to learn. I have been educated in that it is not the projects they are working on that are so important, but the processes that take place during the projects."

Another parent wrote that he had learned the difference between unstructured classrooms and child-centered classrooms, that, at first glance my room can look unstructured, but that with further observation, he found it the most structured room he'd ever seen. The difference was with *who* was doing the structuring. Others said they have learned that age and learning are not necessarily related. One parent wrote, "Children learn at their own pace whether that is at five years or eight years. There is no chronological year they will or are *supposed* to know something."

I also asked if they had noticed any changes outside of school because of what, and how, their child was learning in school. Many parents wrote about the amount of confidence their child had shown outside of school. "Last night, our son walked up to a teenager who had 'borrowed' his inner tube at a local water park and quietly, but firmly, demanded it back. The teenager refused. Our child held his ground and got it back. That kind of behavior was inconceivable a few years ago, and I attribute it in large part to the self-confidence that he has gained from being respected by his teacher, being able to help others learn, and being expected to be self-reliant and learn on his own."

I also asked what concerns, if any, they have about when their child leaves, or has left, the classroom. Many parents expressed concern that their children wouldn't be given enough time to write, and that now that their children had experienced the writing process, they would be subjected to spelling tests and math worksheets. Some were concerned about the social aspects. "My biggest concern is that my son will pick up the negativeness and disrespect between students I have seen in other classrooms. But I feel like he has been given the tools to learn and that he will be able to learn in other environments successfully," one father wrote. Some parents worried that their children wouldn't be respected as individual learners. "My concern would be if an educator later on would stifle or try to direct how my son could learn or lump him into a group when everyone should be individualized," wrote a mother. Another wrote, "My concern is that the teachers in her future are aware of her past learning environment and build upon that. She will do fine, but the most positive transition can be accomplished by everyone working in cooperation with the child's best interest in mind."

I also asked each parent what they would tell other parents who question the program. One parent, whose three children have all been in my classroom, wrote about her youngest child's transition from a traditional kindergarten into my room as a first grader. She wrote, "Last year my daughter was taught writing and reading phonetically. After a couple of weeks she quit writing the stories she loved writing and reading to us. Instead, she began writing only the words she 'knew.' I was upset by this, because I had seen firsthand what can happen if a child is taught the 'correct' way to write and read words. I continued to allow her to write her stories at home the way she did in the past by sounding the words out and letting her know as long as she could read them, they were spelled 'correctly.' After a few months in Jill's class, she was again taking risks with her writing and great stories emerged. I learned that if a child is not allowed to write without worrying about 'correct' spelling, their creativeness is stifled." She went on to write, "Another area where I noticed a problem in her kindergarten class was in math. She did very well when asked what 1 + 1, 2 + 3, even 7 + 7 was, but if you asked her to show it, she didn't know how. So even though she could do the math, she could not explain how she did it." This parent had watched her two other children learn to write by writing and learn math facts by using math facts and explaining how they did it. She explains to other parents why these two aspects of learning are so vital.

Parents also often comment about the level of respect the children in this classroom community have for one another. They have commented about their children's attitudes toward learning. "All three of my children are very different, they have some similarities but a much greater amount of differences. Jill's class has been the best experience for all three of them. They have not only prospered academically, they have gained a greater understanding of how to successfully survive in the real world. The three years each one of them has had in her class will be something they will remember and carry with them throughout their lives. I know I will."

I knew that the parents who answered this survey were positive and supportive of me and my program, but what I didn't know before this survey was how much these parents have learned. I was amazed at what they had learned about development and the learning process. I was struck by how many of their comments were focused on respect, choice, challenge, and independence, and how few were focused on specific skills. Their children had gained confidence—that is apparent from their comments—but I also discovered how much confidence these parents have gained when explaining what they have learned to other parents.

"I suppose another issue that jumps out at me when I enter Jill's room is that of *respect*. The children interact with each other, confident that they will *be* and *do* okay! The respect for oneself and others develops from this constant reaffirmation that each child is who he or she is and *accepted* for whatever that may be!"

What Next?

Epilogue

In May of our island year, I was having a talk with Dave about the following year. "I think we should start at the island and then go somewhere," he said.

"Where should we go? Hey, how about space?" I asked.

"Yeah, maybe. Or, I know!" he said with such excitement, I knew it would be a great idea. "We could start at the island, find this time machine and travel back in time to other places. Like, we could go back to the Civil War time and stuff like that."

"Oh, David, I love that idea! We could go back in American history and learn about America, but also different cultures and how they got here. I love that! We'll have to be sure to bring up this idea at the beginning of the year." A wonderful idea from a seven-year-old that I'd never be able to find in any idea book for teachers.

The island year was coming to a close, and the kids and I knew the next year would be different—every year is different. That's not to say there aren't similarities, or that we couldn't have stayed on the island and just expanded on what we had already done. The kids and I discuss together how we want the year to go. When thinking about the curriculum, the kids just take for granted that they will play a part in creating it. The conversation Dave and I had about the time machine occurred because the kids know they will have a say. These year-long projects seem to be the direction the children and I enjoy going in. Here is a small taste of what we are doing this year.

When September rolled around, we talked about the time/travel machine idea we had discussed in May. We all agreed it would be a great way to plan the year, so we built a time/travel machine, which we call the Time/Travel Chamber. We reused the carpet roll tubes, putting one on each side of our "living room area." Then we strung wire from the top of each tube and draped black flame-proof crepe paper over the entire structure. The couches are inside, and because of the black crepe paper, it makes a nice quiet area.

The kids each made a list of places and time periods they would like to travel to. From these lists, we came up with about fifteen ideas and voted on them. The final itinerary was the Civil War: 1863, the Arctic, and the Future; at the end of the year, each child would be able to go wherever they wanted. I thought it was wonderful of the children to respect Dave's interest in the Civil War and vote it one of our choices.

The Civil War trip went from September to December. It was amazing to observe how much the kids learned about this period. (So much for young children not being able to learn historical information!) We built a covered wagon around our math supply shelves, we made life-sized people from the 1800s out of cardboard, we built wooden toys from the 1800s and put them in our General Store (the platform area), we did various problems, we researched various issues of the period, we dressed up in outfits from the 1800s for Halloween, we created a fictional slave family and "escaped" them on the underground railroad, then had an emancipation celebration for our holiday party, and for the culmination of the "trip," we created a museum with all the things we had done and we invited other classrooms and parents to see it.

The children not only learned basic facts about this historical period, they gained an appreciation for diversity. We had many discussions and read many books on slavery and the African American heritage. Questions such as, "Why would people want to be so mean to other people?" and "Why are most of the characters in books I read white?" and "What color is Santa Claus?" were common. I learned just how much a child is able to absorb. I learned that historical studies are not only possible, they are vital in elementary education, and I learned that I could still stretch myself as an educator.

The children are again in job groups, but they meet much less frequently than in our island year, and usually just before we take off for a new destination.

The jobs directly relate to our Time/Travel study. For instance, one group is called the Collectors. They are responsible for making sure we collect things from all the places we travel to. The Schedule Keepers are in charge of our itinerary.

Because the Civil War "trip" was so successful, I wondered if the kids would want to go to back in time again, but to a different time period, and scrap the Arctic. No way. They insisted on keeping to the schedule. I was quite surprised by this, but since I was outvoted, we will be taking off for the Arctic next. The only plan we have so far is to transform the covered wagon into the entryway of an ice house. I know I want the kids to study about the people who live in different regions of the Arctic, but other than that, I'll just have to wait and see where this trip leads us.

What about next year? Who knows. Maybe the kids will want to continue with the Time/Travel idea, maybe they'll want to go back to the island, or maybe we will do something completely different. What will remain the same, no matter what we do or where we go, will be the importance of choice, challenge, independence, and respect.

References

Professional Resources

Atwell, Nancie. 1987. *In the Middle: Writing, Reading, and Learning with Adolescents.* Portsmouth, NH: Heinemann.

Austin, Terri. 1994. *Changing the View: Student-led Parent Conferences.* Portsmouth, NH: Heinemann.

Burk, Donna, and Allyn Snider. 1994. *Posing and Solving Problems with Storyboxes.* Salem, OR: The Math Learning Center.

Burns, Marilyn. 1994. *About Teaching Mathematics.* White Plains, NY: Cuisenaire.

Countryman, Joan. 1992. *Writing to Learn Mathematics.* Portsmouth, NH: Heinemann.

Ernst, Karen. 1993. *Picturing Learning: Artists and Writers in the Classroom.* Portsmouth, NH: Heinemann.

Goodman, Kenneth S. 1986. *What's Whole in Whole Language?* Portsmouth, NH: Heinemann.

Graves, Donald H. 1983. *Writing: Children and Teachers at Work.* Portsmouth, NH: Heinemann.

Hansen, Jane, Thomas Newkirk, and Donald H. Graves. 1985. *Breaking Ground: Teachers Relate Reading and Writing in the Elementary School.* Portsmouth, NH: Heinemann.

Hubbard, Ruth. 1995. *A Workshop of the Possible.* York, ME: Stenhouse.

Hubbard, Ruth, and Brenda M. Power. 1991. *Literacy in Process: The Heinemann Reader.* Portsmouth, NH: Heinemann.

Taylor, Denny. 1991. *Learning Denied.* Portsmouth, NH: Heinemann.

Wilde, Sandra. 1993. *You Kan Red This! Spelling and Punctuation for Whole Language Classrooms, K-6.* Portsmouth, NH: Heinemann.

Children's Books

Alexander, Lloyd. 1978. *The Book of Three.* New York: Dell.

Belanger, Claude. 1988. *The Dog.* Illus. by Mary Davy. Auckland, NZ: Shortland.

Burnett, Frances H. 1989. *The Secret Garden.* New York: Dell.

Dahl, Roald. 1984. *James and the Giant Peach.* New York: Bantam.

———. 1991. *The MinPins.* Illus. by Patrick Benson. New York: Penguin.

Dixon, Franklin. *The Hardy Boys.* New York: Simon & Schuster.

Lewis, C. S. 1988. *The Lion, the Witch, and the Wardrobe.* Illus. by Pauline Baynes. New York: Macmillan.

Lobel, Arnold. *Frog and Toad.* New York: HarperCollins.

MacLachlan, Patricia. 1985. *Sarah, Plain and Tall.* New York: HarperCollins.

Minarik, Else H. 1986. *Little Bear.* Illus. by Maurice Sendak. New York: Harper & Row.

Tolkien, J. R. R. 1989. *The Hobbit.* Illus. by Michael Hague. Boston: Houghton Mifflin.

Index

physical environment
  problems, 42–43
  transforming, 9–17
Picturing Learning (Ernst), 46
planetarium, 35–36
planning commission, 21–22
platforms, 32
plotting to scale, Garden Problem,
  104–5
poetry, 55
ponds, 37–38
Pongol (India), 79–80
Portfolio Assessment, 124, 126
portfolios
  for assessment, 124–26
  for conferences, 130–31
  cumulative, 125–26
  Pass-On Portfolios, 125–26
  Portfolio Assessment, 124, 126
  Working Portfolio, 124–25
*Posing and Solving Problems with Story-
  boxes* (Burk and Snider), 68
presentations
  Garden Problem, 102–4
  Journey Problem, 87–89
  multicultural holidays, 78–79
  skit format, 89
  student evaluation of, 102–4
  talk show format, 89
problems, designing for children, 75–76
problem-solving
  independence in, 107–9
  Math Workshop, 65–66
  in multi-age classrooms, 91–92
  sharing, 93
progress
  measuring, 113–17
  in reading, 60–62
progress wheels, 113–17
  Progress as an Independent Learner,
  115–17

Progress as a Community Learner,
  115–17

Quiet Writing, 40–41

reading
  improvement programs, 60–62, 136
  strategies, 58
Reading Recovery, 60–62
Reading Workshop, 57–64
  assessing during, 113
  choice, 57–58
  Literature Groups, 58–60
  music in, 39
  progress, 60–62
  scheduling, 45
  sharing, 62–63
  strategies, 63–64
reflections, writing about Garden Problem, 101–2
research, multicultural holidays, 77–78
"resource kids," 26
respect, 62, 140, 141
  sense of community and, 5, 117
responsibility, for cleaning up, 43
revision, 50–51
  checksheet, 51–52
rewriting, 53
rubrics, 103, 126

seating, assigned, 30–31
self-assessment, 102, 130–31
self-confidence, 139, 140
sharing
  ideas, 17
  problem-solving, 93
  Reading Workshop, 62–63
skills, Math Workshop, 65
Snider, Allyn, 7, 40, 65, 68, 121
snow festivals, 80
socializing, 30

Also of Interest

A Workshop of the Possible
Nurturing Children's Creative Development
Ruth Shagoury Hubbard

Ruth Hubbard has spent the last ten years researching in classrooms, documenting what children can do and how teachers can create classroom environments that promote children's many strengths.

Drawing on examples from Jill Ostrow's classes, Ruth Hubbard shows how teachers can develop children's creativity in classrooms that respect their amazing abilities. This book is especially valuable for those teachers who want to integrate a child-centered curriculum beyond reading and writing. While grounded in holistic and constructivist literacy theory, it goes beyond language arts into math and science, into children conducting research and problem-solving.

Teachers will appreciate the numerous examples from inside classrooms, stressing issues that teachers and students confront and grapple with, and problems that arise and must be solved. At the heart of the book are the voices of the children themselves as informants and samples of the inspiring work they have produced.

1-57110-007-5   Paperback

Exploring the Multiage Classroom
Anne A. Bingham

Teachers who are planning to move into multiage or have already made that transition from a conventional classroom, will welcome the honest, practical advice that makes this a genuine handbook—comprehensive, realistic, and accessible. Anne Bingham demonstrates clearly what teachers find rewarding in multiage teaching and why it works so well for children who can learn from the models provided by the literacy and learning of other children around them.

Grounded in the relevant philosophy, research, and theory, *Exploring the Multiage Classroom* is a treasury of ideas derived from the author's wide classroom experience. She shares details on working effectively with groups and individuals, adapting the curriculum to a multiage setting, and full chapters on integrated themes, oral language, student choice, literacy, math, assessment, moving into a multiage organization, and teaming. The book also includes appendices that provide a classroom materials list, sample schedules, room layouts, and bibliographies of professional resources and children's books.

1-57110-013-X   Paperback